SynDEVS Co-Design Flow

H. Gregor Molter

SynDEVS Co-Design Flow

A Hardware / Software Co-Design Flow
Based on the Discrete Event System
Specification Model of Computation

 Springer Vieweg   **RESEARCH**

H. Gregor Molter
Darmstadt, Germany

Dissertation Technische Universität Darmstadt

D 17

ISBN 978-3-658-00396-8   ISBN 978-3-658-00397-5 (eBook)
DOI 10.1007/978-3-658-00397-5

Library of Congress Control Number: 2012950144

The Deutsche Nationalbibliothek lists this publication in the Deutsche Nationalbibliografie; detailed bibliographic data are available in the Internet at http://dnb.d-nb.de.

Springer Vieweg
© Springer Fachmedien Wiesbaden 2012

Printed on acid-free paper

Springer Vieweg is a brand of Springer DE. Springer DE is part of Springer Science+Business Media.
www.springer-vieweg.de

This thesis is dedicated to my parents.

 " A journey of a thousand miles begins with a single step. "

Ancient Chinese Philosopher 老子 *(Lǎo zǐ)*
6th century B.C.E.

Acknowledgements

This thesis was written during my time at the *Integrated Circuits and Systems Lab* at the Technische Universität Darmstadt, Germany. No thesis will be carried out in isolation – and this particular one is certainly no exception. The opinions and constructive criticism of many people have influenced this thesis.

I am deeply grateful to Prof. Dr.-Ing. Sorin A. Huss, for his open mindedness to my ideas, for the constructive discussions about my thesis' topic, for being an excellent supervisor and especially for making this all possible.

I am very thankful to Prof. Dr.-Ing. Jürgen Teich, for his interest in my work and for refereeing this thesis.

I would like to thank all my colleagues at the Integrated Circuits and Systems Lab, Tolga Arul, Tom Assmuth, Alexander Biedermann, Lijing Chen, Thomas Feller, Annelie Heuser, Adeel Israr, Attila Jaeger, Michael Jung, Ralf Laue, Zheng Lu, Felix Madlener, Sunil Malipatlolla, Tim Sander, André Seffrin, Abdulhadi Shoufan, Marc Stöttinger, Hagen Stübing, Qizhi Tian, and Michael Zohner, for all their scientific support.

I would like to give a special thanks to Maria Tiedemann for her ongoing support of our group and for always giving a helping hand.

This thesis would not have been possible without the support of the students, Steven Arzt, Martin Feldmann, Yanmin Guo, Nico Huber, Johannes Kohlmann, Eike Kohnert, Robert Mahs, Daniel Münch, Kiril Nastev, Kei Ogata, Felix Rieder, Gregor Rynkowski, Kartik Saxena, Nabil Sayegh, Michael Schaffner, Hui Shao, Alexander Spitzl, and Thorsten Wink. Thank you for your great effort!

At the end, I would like to give some very special thanks to my parents and to my fiancée Simone Reinhart, for your love and help, for your support over the years, and for just being there when I need you.

H. Gregor Molter

Zusammenfassung

Die Komplexität von modernen eingebetteten Systemen hat stark zugenommen in den letzten Jahren. Daher wurde die Abstraktion im Systementwurf durch die Einführung von Berechenbarkeitsmodellen im Entwurfsprozess erhöht. Die Anwendung solch hoch abstrakter Methoden in gängigen Hard- und Software Ko-Entwurfsabläufen steckt noch in den Kinderschuhen. Die meisten Synthese-Werkzeuge aus der Industrie und Forschung benutzen Berechenbarkeitsmodelle alleinig für einen kleinen Teil der anfallenden Entwurfsaufgaben.

Ein Hard- und Software Ko-Entwurfsablauf basierend auf dem Discrete Event System Specification (DEVS) Berechenbarkeitsmodell ist der Hauptbeitrag dieser Dissertation. Es wird vorgeschlagen, dass solch ein Entwurfsablauf ein zeitgesteuertes Berechenbarkeitsmodell benutzen sollte um das Anwendungsgebiet zu vergrößern. Der präsentierte Entwurfsablauf transformiert zeitgesteuerte DEVS-Modelle sowohl in synthesierbaren VHDL Quellcode als auch eingebetteten C++ Quellcode. Während des Entwurfsablaufs werden automatisierte Modelloptimierungen bzgl. des Zeitverhaltens vorgenommen und Kommunikationsschnittstellen zwischen den Hard- und Software Anteilen generiert. Zusätzlich wird aufgezeigt, wie bestehender C / C++ Quellcode eingebunden werden kann, so dass keine angereicherte Plattform-abhängige Fachkompetenz verloren geht. Dies ist besonders wichtig bei der Einführung von Berechenbarkeitsmodellen in den Entwurfsablauf eingebetteter Systeme, da die Entwicklung solcher Systeme ein evolutionärer Prozess ist. Ferner wird eine frühzeitige Simulation des Systems anhand von SystemC beschrieben.

Um die Machbarkeit der vorgeschlagenen Methodik zu demonstrieren, wurde eine graphische Anwendung zum Modellentwurf und zur Modellanalyse entwickelt. Die Verhaltensbeschreibung der Modelle kann daher graphisch festgelegt werden. Alle Teilschritte des Entwurfsablaufs können über die Anwendung ausgeführt werden. Jeder Entwurfsschritt erzeugt hierbei ein verfeinertes Modell des Originalmodells, welches komplett in der Anwendung nachbearbeitet werden kann.

Die Dissertation schließt mit drei Fallbeispielen ab, wobei jedes Beispiel unterschiedliche Aspekte der vorgeschlagenen Methodik hervorhebt.

Abstract

The complexity of modern embedded systems increased rapidly in the recent past. Thus, the abstraction in system level design of embedded systems was significantly raised by introducing Models of Computation (MoCs) into the design flow. Establishing such high abstraction levels in common hardware / software co-design flows is still in its infancy. Most academic and industrial synthesis tools available on the market feature an exploitation of MoCs only for a small subset of the required system level design tasks.

The main contribution of this thesis is a hardware / software co-design flow based on Discrete Event System Specification (DEVS) Model of Computation (MoC). It is advocated that such a system level design flow has to exploit a timed MoC to allow a broad application field. The presented design flow will transform timed DEVS models to both synthesizable VHDL source code and embeddable C++ source code. During the design flow, automated model optimization in terms of timing requirements and automated communication interface generation for hardware / software co-design will be exploited. Additionally, legacy C / C++ source code reuse is highlighted, which allows for the integration of previously aggregated platform-dependent expertise. This is of utmost importance for the introduction of MoCs into the embedded systems design flow, because development of such systems is in general an evolutionary process. Furthermore, early simulation of the system design using SystemC is described.

To demonstrate the feasibility of the advocated methodology, a Graphical User Interface (GUI) featuring model creation and model review was developed. As a best-practice approach, the designer of the system may specify the model behaviour in terms of exploiting a visual programming paradigm. All different design flow tasks may be centrally controlled using the GUI. Every intermediate step of the design flow results is a refined model of the original system itself, which may be reviewed within the GUI.

The thesis concludes with three case studies highlighting the different aspects and benefits of the advocated methodology.

Contents

List of Figures

List of Tables

List of Algorithms and Listings

Acronyms

AST	Abstract Syntax Tree
BC	Border Channel
BNF	Backus-Naur Form
BP	Border Process
BRAM	Block RAM
CSP	Communicating Sequential Processes
CT	Continuous Time
DE	Discrete Event
DEVS	Discrete Event System Specification
DSP	Digital Signal Processing
DVI	Digital Visual Interface
E^2PROM	Electrically Erasable Programmable Read-Only Memory
ECC	Elliptic Curve Cryptography
ECDSA	Elliptic Curve Digital Signature Algorithm
EDA	Electronic Design Automation
EDIF	Electronic Design Interchange Format
EDK	Embedded Development Kit
ESL	Electronic System Level
FPGA	Field Programmable Gate Array
FSL	Fast-Simplex-Link
FSM	Finite State Machine
GUI	Graphical User Interface
HLA	High Level Architecture
I^2C	Inter-Integrated Circuit; generically referred to as *two-wire interface*
IP	Intellectual Property
ISE	Integrated Synthesis Environment
ISR	Interrupt Service Routine
KPN	Kahn Process Network
LMB	Local Memory Bus
LUT	Lookup Table

MoC	Model of Computation
NoC	Network on a chip
OSCI	Open SystemC Initiative
PBC	Pairing-Based Cryptography
PC	Program Counter
PCIe	Peripheral Component Interconnect Express
PLB	Processor Local Bus
ROM	Read-Only Memory
RSA	Rivest, Shamir, and Adleman; a public key encryption technology
RTL	Register Transfer Level
RTOS	Real-time Operating System
SCXML	State Chart XML
SoC	System on a chip
SPU	Special Purpose Unit
SR	Synchronous Reactive
SynDEVS	Synthesizable DEVS
SysML	Systems Modelling Language
TFT	Thin-Film Transistor
TLM	Transaction-Level Modelling
UART	Universal Asynchronous Receiver Transmitter
UML	Unified Modelling Language
VHDL	Very High Speed Integrated Circuit Hardware Description Language
XML	Extensible Markup Language

CHAPTER 1

Introduction

In the recent years, the complexity of modern embedded systems is increasing rapidly. Embedded systems exploited only a single or only a few micro-controllers in their infancy. Nowadays, these highly complex systems feature diverse multi-core processor architectures. Even more, embedded systems may exploit SoC[1] or NoC[2] platforms which arose lately on the market. Thus, today's embedded systems are truly heterogeneous systems with strict real-time requirements. Hence, the term *cyber physical systems* is gaining more and more momentum in favour of the term *embedded systems* for those architectures, because a system embedded in a physical world requires time as an inherent system property. Cyber physical systems demand for a design methodology which is aware of time in both hardware and software domains.

Traditional hardware / software co-design approaches require a lot of effort to get the different counterparts of the system working together seamlessly. Usually, these heterogeneous systems are specified by hardware description languages (e.g. VHDL[3]) and software languages (e.g. C), which are not well aware of their hardware or software counterpart. Even more, established software languages such as C, C++, or Java, which are usually exploited within embedded systems, have no appropriate means for defining time within. Thus, the system level design of such systems with traditional hardware and software languages is an error-prone process, which is bound tightly to the exploited architecture.

Intellectual property (e.g. VHDL source code) is often manually optimized for specific target architectures to increase performance and, thus, cannot be easily deployed into different architectures. A new target ar-

---

[1] *System on a chip*

[2] *Network on a chip*

[3] *Very High Speed Integrated Circuit Hardware Description Language*

chitecture often requires a restructure of the system partitioning into its hardware and its software components to meet application requirements. For instance, software algorithms have to be shifted to hardware to meet timing constraints and, thus, the software which is presumably written in C source code has to be transformed to an appropriate hardware module specified using a hardware description language such as VHDL. Taken together, these common hardware / software co-design approaches are not suitable any more for the current demands of cyber physical systems. Therefore, abstraction of system level design has been raised by exploiting MoCs[4] within the design flow.

1.1 Models of Computation

MoCs allow us to step back from the platform-dependent implementation of a cyber physical system to a more abstract view of the system and its designated behaviour. By exploiting a diversity of MoCs with each having specific properties, different system level design problems may be tackled. For instance, an algorithm which will be modelled with a Petri net may be verified for the Petri net property of liveness. This property implies that the algorithm always terminates and, thus, no deadlock will occur during the execution. Another benefit of using MoCs is the reusability: Once domain specific expertise is gained within a MoC, it will not be lost across different target-platforms. Hence, an embedded system level design flow should be built upon exploitation of diverse MoCs, but a solely use of a single MoC will be extremely beneficial compared to a common hardware / software co-design flow based on C and VHDL. Specifically, an exploitation of a timed MoC is the most promising approach regarding the system level design of cyber physical systems.

A lot of scientific effort has been put into the research of MoCs in respect of an embedded system level design flow. In the following, the most prominent ones are shortly discussed and reviewed in terms of their applicability for an hardware / software co-design flow based on MoCs.

ForSyDe [SJ04] is a functional programming framework with synthesizable code generation. The design process starts with an abstract formal specification model of the system which is required to be perfectly synchronous. Synthesizable code generation is a two step process: First, the

---

[4] *Models of Computation*

initial abstract model will be successively refined by applying transformations until a more detailed implementable model is reached. Second, this implementation model will be mapped to the target architecture by exploiting hardware / software co-design algorithms like partitioning, resource allocation, and generation of C source code and VHDL source code. However, the modelling fidelity is limited in terms of the initial assumption of perfect synchronicity. This assumption may not be fulfilled by the computational models of a broad application field.

In contrast, Ptolemy II [BLL$^+$05] is a genuine multi-MoC design environment. It is a pure simulation and modelling environment for heterogeneous systems exploiting a diversity of MoCs (e.g. FSM[5], DE[6], CT[7], CSP[8], or KPN[9]). In [FLN06], limited hardware synthesis of Ptolemy II model is introduced, which is primarily suitable for DSP applications because transformations of models are only allowed from the SR[10] domain to VHDL.

HetSC [HV07] ease the software implementation of heterogeneous MoC designs. The employed models may be manually refined into synthesizable SystemC source code. Hence, it does not feature an automatic transformation of the whole MoC. However, together with ANDRES [HV07], it is strong in both, software transformation and hardware synthesis, but different MoCs will be exploited for the hardware and the software parts of the system under consideration. Thus, domain specific knowledge aggregated within one of these MoCs may not be easily transferred to the other. Therefore, MoC specific properties may be lost during design space exploration, model refinement, and especially during hardware / software co-design.

A comprehensive list of platform-based industrial and academic system level design tools is given in [DP06]. This survey results in the fact that, firstly, only a small subset of tools consider timed MoCs, and secondly, these cover only a small subset of the tasks necessary for synthesis. Thus, no complete system level design flow exploiting a single, timed MoC is covered.

In this thesis, a systematic approach of integrating diverse MoCs into a system level design flow in terms of model transformations will be pre-

---

[5] *Finite State Machine*

[6] *Discrete Event*

[7] *Continuous Time*

[8] *Communicating Sequential Processes*

[9] *Kahn Process Network*

[10] *Synchronous Reactive*

sented. Then, the advocated hardware/software co-design flow will exploit only a single timed MoC to accomplish hardware synthesis and software implementation. Therefore, the well-known timed DEVS[11] MoC from Zeigler et al. [ZKP00] will be exploited as a foundation for the system level design flow.

1.2 DEVS Model of Computation

The DEVS formalism is a strong mathematical foundation for specifying hierarchical, concurrently executed formal models. It covers both time-discrete and time-continuous models. However, this thesis focus on the time-discrete operation only.

A lot of scientific effort has been put into research the DEVS MoC. For instance, the generation of a reachability graph is given in [HZ09]. In [Wai09], plenty of real-world simulation application examples are given for the DEVS formalism which has its roots in the simulation domain. Interoperability with another other MoC (i.e. UML[12]) in terms of model transformations is presented in [RMZ+07] for UML state charts or in [SV11] for UML class diagrams, just to name a few.

However, the original time-discrete DEVS MoC has some inherent properties which impede direct synthesis of the models. For instance, an output port may emit an unbound amount of events within a single point in time. Such a behaviour is clearly not synthesizable because it would possibly require an infinite amount of memory at the sink to process these emitted events. Thus, the original formalism is refined in this thesis and presented in a much clearer behaviour definition named SynDEVS[13] MoC which allows synthesis.

The refined version was carefully constructed with the following basic principles in mind:

- Substantiate the DEVS MoC behaviour to allow synthesis.

- If a DEVS model is synthesizable in terms of not exploiting the non-synthesizable DEVS properties, then it has to be possible to transform the original model easily into an equivalent synthesizable SynDEVS model.

---

[11] *Discrete Event System Specification*
[12] *Unified Modelling Language*
[13] *Synthesizable DEVS*

- Preserving as much as possible of the original DEVS properties is of utmost importance.

Additionally, the transformation of SynDEVS models to hardware and software will be detailed in this thesis. Therefore, the models of the timed SynDEVS MoC will be transformed into synthesizable VHDL source code and embeddable C++ source code. By doing so, the system may be designed in an abstract manner by using MoCs, but existing synthesis software and compilers supplied by the target platform vendors may be still exploited. Hence, such an approach allows for an easy use of SynDEVS MoC within an existing embedded system design flow. Thus, there is no need of re-modelling the whole system with SynDEVS but instead the MoC may be only partially exploited where it is beneficial for the system. By doing so, once gained platform-dependent knowledge (e.g. a well-evaluated network stack source code library) is not lost. Thus, the transition to a solely use of MoCs within the design flow may be performed over time. This reflects the design process of embedded systems which is in general an evolutionary process.

1.3 Hardware / Software Co-Design Flow

In this thesis, a hardware / software co-design flow based on the DEVS MoC will be presented. Figure 1.1 depicts this abstract system level design flow. The figure will be reused at each chapter relevant to the design flow, only highlighting the topics covered in the chapter.

The abstract DEVS-based design flow may be exploited to create implementable models. Thus, automatic transformations down to abstraction levels covering VHDL synthesis and embedded systems C++ executable source code generation are included. The designer may supply DEVS models either by creating them with a developed GUI[14] and/or by the (automated) transformation of different domain-specific MoCs into DEVS models. Simulation and Verification may be exploited to test models for correct behaviour. Therefore, the DEVS models may be simulated with a non-introspective SystemC™ kernel extension. Verification may be done by applying the work from Madlener et al. [MWH10] which exploits an automatic model transformation into UPPAAL model-checker verification models.

---

[14] *Graphical User Interface*

Figure 1.1 DEVS design flow covered by this thesis, highlighting different topics in terms of design entry, simulation, and hardware / software co-design. Throughout the thesis, at the beginning of each chapter relevant to the design flow, this figure will be shown, only highlighting the topics covered in the chapter.

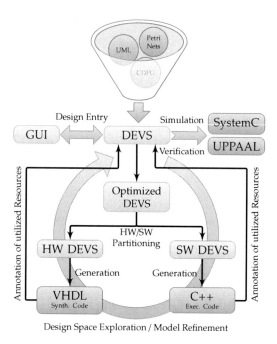

Design Space Exploration / Model Refinement

At any time during the system level design, the designer may execute the following fully automated design flow process: First, the input model covering the whole system is optimized regarding different timing aspects and the model's component hierarchy is flattened. Second, the flattened and optimized system level model is split into a single SynDEVS model each for the hardware and software generation processes of the design flow. Communication interfaces in between the hardware and software instances may be automatically generated. Design space exploration and model refinement will be supported in terms of back-annotating the utilized resources to the initial model. Every intermediate model of the design flow will be a SynDEVS model, too. Thus, the designer has full control over each step in the design flow to further refine the model. This approach of a fully transparent design flow is very beneficial for more sophisticated design space exploration methods not covered in this thesis. These may be easily introduced by writing further (automated) tools which may operate on these intermediate SynDEVS models.

1.4 Remainder of this Thesis

The original DEVS formalism will be reviewed and discussed in terms of synthesis in Chapter 2. A revised version of the formalism in order to support synthesis will be introduced. This SynDEVS MoC will be defined and reviewed in detail in terms of synthesis aspects. Additionally, a visual notation of the SynDEVS model will be introduced.

Chapter 3 will present modelling and validation methods of SynDEVS MoC. First, it will be discussed how diverse MoCs may be transformed into SynDEVS MoC. Second, the validation of SynDEVS models in terms of SystemC simulation will be presented.

Afterwards, the main contribution of this thesis, the advocated hardware / software co-design flow based on SynDEVS MoC will be introduced. First, Hardware / Software partitioning will be detailed. Second, both model transformations to synthesizable VHDL source code and embeddable C++ source code will be thoroughly discussed. It will be detailed how SynDEVS timing annotations are implemented within the resulting VHDL and C++ source codes. An optimization algorithm will be introduced which generates a SynDEVS model with equivalent behaviour but with improved timing constraints. Furthermore, integration of legacy C / C++ source code software libraries into the SynDEVS software instances will be detailed.

Chapter 5 will shortly introduce the developed GUI for the SynDEVS MoC. The complete design flow may be centrally controlled using the GUI. Furthermore, all intermediate models of the design flow may be reviewed within the GUI.

In the following Chapter 6, three case studies will be presented. Each case study highlights different parts of the design flow: A SynDEVS model of a DVI[15] controller with strict real-time requirements will be discussed highlighting the hardware part of the design flow. Then, this DVI controller will be extended to implement a network-based Pong game in order to demonstrate the software part of the design flow with legacy source code integration. Afterwards, a flexible cryptographic accelerator will be introduced to show the benefits of partially exploiting SynDEVS MoC within an existing design.

Finally, Chapter 7 concludes this thesis. Important points will be summarized and an outlook for further research challenges will be given.

---

[15] *Digital Visual Interface*

CHAPTER 2

Discrete Event System Specification

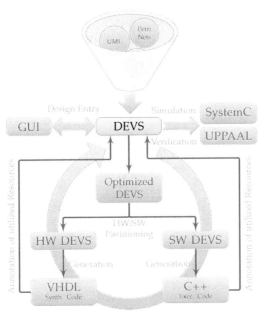

In this chapter, the classic DEVS formalism from Zeigler et al. will be introduced. It will be discussed in depth, which properties of the DEVS MoC impedes its exploitation for a hardware / software co-design flow. Thus, the SynDEVS MoC will be introduced which thoroughly refines the DEVS MoC to allow synthesis of SynDEVS models. At the end of this chapter, a graphical notation will be presented which is very beneficial regarding the readability of a model in contrast to the original pure mathematical notation.

2.1 Classic DEVS with Ports and Parallel DEVS Coupled Models

The DEVS formalism for discrete event systems introduced by Zeigler et al. in [ZKP00] is a strong mathematical foundation for specifying hierarchically, concurrently executed formal models. It affords a computational basis for specifying the behaviour of such models in a clear simplified manner. Zeigler et al. specified the so-called Classic DEVS with Ports, a structure for describing single, sequentially executed, timed automata for discrete event systems. Afterwards, this concept was further developed to cope with recent developments of computer architectures (i.e. the increasing degree of parallelization). Parallel DEVS Coupled Models was introduced allowing the modelling of concurrently executed, hierarchically, timed automata for discrete event systems. As a result, the Classic DEVS with Ports was embedded into Parallel DEVS Coupled Models by means of atomic components and will be detailed later on in Subsection 2.1.2. However, before discussing the atomic components, which implement the behaviour of the models, the Parallel DEVS in terms of parallel components will be introduced in the following section.

2.1.1 Parallel Components

Parallel components within DEVS allow to model hierarchies of concurrently executed components. A parallel component interconnects atomic or other parallel components with its input and output ports. Thus, a parallel component is a 8-tuple

$$\text{DEVS}_{\text{parallel}} = (P_{\text{in}}, P_{\text{out}}, X, Y, M, C_{\text{in}}, C_{\text{out}}, C_{\text{inner}}).$$

Parallel components have a finite set of input ports P_{in} and output ports P_{out}. Further, each port has its own event value set defined in $X_{p \in P_{in}} \in X$ (input port event value sets) and $Y_{p \in P_{out}} \in Y$ (output port event value sets).

The inner components M of a parallel component may be either other parallel components or atomic components. Additionally, inner components may be coupled with the input and output ports of each other or with the parallel component itself.

The sets C_{in}, C_{out}, and C_{inner} specify port couplings of input ports and inner components (C_{in}), output ports and inner components (C_{out}), and in between inner components (C_{inner}). A port coupling is a pair of component and port tuples, i.e.

$$((c_{source}, p_{source}), (c_{destination}, p_{destination})).$$

The source and destination components c_{source} and $c_{destination}$ are either inner components or the parallel component itself, i.e.

$$c_{source}, c_{destination} \in M \cup \{DEVS_{parallel}\}.$$

The source port p_{source} has to be an input or output port of the component c_{source}, i.e.

$$p_{source} \in \begin{cases} P_{out} \text{ of } c_{source} & \text{if } c_{source} \in M \\ P_{in} \text{ of } c_{source} & \text{if } c_{source} = DEVS_{parallel}. \end{cases}$$

Similarly, the destination port $p_{destination}$ has to be an output or input port of the component $c_{destination}$, i.e.

$$p_{destination} \in \begin{cases} P_{in} \text{ of } c_{destination} & \text{if } c_{destination} \in M \\ P_{out} \text{ of } c_{destination} & \text{if } c_{destination} = DEVS_{parallel}. \end{cases}$$

Thus, only port couplings between an event source and drain are allowed. An event source (drain) is either an output (input) port of an inner component or the input (output) port of the parallel component itself. Except this simple but generic rule of data-flow architectures, i.e., data-flow is represented as a data-dependent digraph [DFL74], port couplings are almost unconstrained. However, port couplings in terms of direct feedback loops are not allowed as well. Thus, output and input ports of the same component (i.e. $c_{source} = c_{destination}$) may not be connected together.

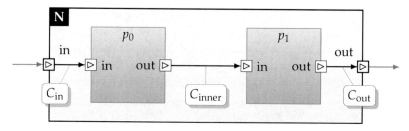

Figure 2.1 Parallel component example with two inner atomic components

Example

Figure 2.1 depicts an example of two coupled atomic components within a parallel component. The parallel component N is

$$N = (P_{in}, P_{out}, X, Y, M, C_{in}, C_{out}, C_{inner})$$

where

$$
\begin{aligned}
P_{in} &= \{"in"\} \\
P_{out} &= \{"out"\} \\
P_{in,in} &= V \text{ (an arbitary set of values)} \\
P_{out,out} &= V \\
M &= \{(p_0, A), (p_1, A)\} \text{ (A is another component definition)} \\
C_{in} &= \{((N, "in"), (p_0, "in"))\} \\
C_{out} &= \{((p_1, "out"), (N, "out"))\} \\
C_{inner} &= \{((p_0, "out"), (p_1, "in"))\} .
\end{aligned}
$$

2.1.2 Atomic Components

An atomic component implements the models behaviour in terms of a finite state machine with timed state transitions. It is denoted by an 11-tuple

$$\text{DEVS}_{atomic} = (P_{in}, P_{out}, X, Y, S, s_0, \delta_{int}, \delta_{ext}, \delta_{con}, \lambda, \tau).$$

Atomic components have a finite set of input ports P_{in} to receive events and output ports P_{out} to emit events. Likewise the parallel component ports,

Figure 2.2 Relation of internal state transition and output function execution in DEVS atomic components

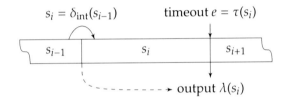

$$s_i = \delta_{\text{int}}(s_{i-1}) \qquad \text{timeout } e = \tau(s_i)$$

each port has its own event value set defined in $X_{p \in P_{\text{in}}} \in X$ (input port event value sets) and $Y_{p \in P_{\text{out}}} \in Y$ (output port event value sets).

S is a non-empty set of states. The initial state of the atomic component is $s_0 \in S \cap \{\emptyset\}$. Every state $s \in S$ has an associated timeout value $\tau(s)$ with $\tau : S \rightarrow \mathbb{R}^+$ describing the maximum retention time of the state. Hence, timeout values can be assigned into three timing classes depicted by Table 2.1.

These different timing classes are of particular interest regarding the models state change and output behaviour. Whenever a model stayed in a state for the duration defined by $\tau(s)$ a timeout event occur and a state change is performed. Then, the internal transition function $\delta_{\text{int}} : S \rightarrow S$ is executed determining the successor state $s' = \delta_{\text{int}}(s)$ of the current state s with $s, s' \in S$. Furthermore, the model may emit a single output event described by the function $\lambda : S \rightarrow Y^b$. Please note that Y^b is a set of all possible output event values $Y_{p \in P_{\text{out}}}$ where multiple occurrences of the same symbol are allowed, i.e. $y \in Y^b$ is a bag y containing all emitted output events. Figure 2.2 depicts the relation between the internal state transition and the output function execution within atomic components in DEVS. After entering the state s_i its output value $\lambda(s_i)$ is determined. Afterwards, the calculated value is emitted when the state is left due to a timeout event. Please note that a model may emit multiple output events at the same point in time, due to the zero-timeout of states. All output events which occur in zero-timeout states are collected within a bag and, afterwards, they are simultaneously transmitted altogether.

A state change is also performed when an input event is received. Then,

Table 2.1 Different timing classes of the state timeout function τ

Timing Class	Set of timing values $\subset \mathbb{R}^+$
Zero-timeout	$\{0\}$
Real-timeout	$\mathbb{R}^+ \setminus \{0, \infty\}$
Non-timeout	$\{\infty\}$

the external transition function $\delta_{ext} : S \times X \times \mathbb{R}^+ \to S$ is executed. Thus, whatever event (*timeout* or *external*) occurs first, the corresponding transition function is executed and the state change is performed within the atomic component. However, for the special case that at the same point in time, both, input and timeout events occur, it is not decidable whether the internal or external transition function should be executed. In such a case the target state cannot be properly computed.

Zeigler et al. introduced in [ZKP00] an additional transition function to circumvent this DEVS MoC design flaw: The confluent transition function $\delta_{con} : S \times X \times \mathbb{R}^+ \to S$. This function is executed whenever this special case occur and, thus, making the model's state change behaviour decidable. Taken together, the successor state s' is determined by

$$s' = \begin{cases} \delta_{int}(s) & \text{if } e = \tau(s) \\ \delta_{ext}(s, x, e) & \text{if at least a single input event occured and } e \neq \tau(s) \\ \delta_{con}(s, x, e) & \text{otherwise.} \end{cases}$$

In addition, δ_{con} can be classified by three fundamentally different kinds of confluent transition functions:

$$\delta_{con}(s, x, e) = \begin{cases} \delta_{int}(s) \text{ or } \delta_{ext}(s, x, e) & \text{(Type 1)} \\ \delta_{int}(\delta_{ext}(s, x, e)) \text{ or } \delta_{ext}(\delta_{int}(s), x, e) & \text{(Type 2)} \\ f(s, x, e). & \text{(Type 3)} \end{cases}$$

Type 1 confluent transition functions globally decide which event (i.e. internal or external event) is irrelevant and should not be processed at all. Type 2 functions globally decide which event has a higher priority and should be processed in favour. Type 3 functions are the common case where the successor state can be freely defined without reusing the existing δ_{int} or δ_{ext} functions of the model. Taken together, Type 1 is embedded within Type 2 and Type 3. Likewise, Type 2 is embedded in Type 3. Thus, it is Type 1 $\subset$ Type 2 $\subset$ Type 3. Please note that each δ_{con} type has an increasing design complexity but allows higher expressiveness of the model in comparison to the preceding subtype.

Example

A simple atomic component is shown below. The model receives an event with value n from its input port and calculate within 5 ns an output event

Figure 2.3 Trajectories for the example atomic DEVS model M. Input and output events are shown in relation to the model state.

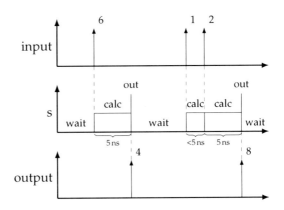

with value $10 - n$. The atomic component M is

$$M = (P_{in}, P_{out}, X, Y, S, s_0, \delta_{int}, \delta_{ext}, \delta_{con}, \lambda, \tau)$$

where

$$
\begin{aligned}
P_{in} &= \{\text{"input"}\} \\
P_{out} &= \{\text{"output"}\} \\
P_{in,input} &= \{0, 1, 2, 3, 4, 5, 6, 7, 8, 9, 10\} \\
P_{out,output} &= P_{in,input} \\
S &= \{\text{wait, calc, out}\} \times P_{in,input} \\
s_0 &= (\text{wait}, 0) \\
\delta_{int}((\tilde{s}, n)) &= \begin{cases} (\text{out}, n) & \text{if } \tilde{s} = \text{calc} \\ (\text{wait}, n) & \text{otherwise} \end{cases} \\
\delta_{ext}((\tilde{s}, n), x, e) &= \begin{cases} (\text{calc}, x) & \text{if } \tilde{s} = \text{wait} \\ (\tilde{s}, x) & \text{otherwise} \end{cases} \\
\delta_{con}(s, x, e) &= \delta_{ext}(\delta_{int}(s), x, e) \\
\lambda((\text{out}, n)) &= 10 - n \\
\tau((\tilde{s}, n)) &= \begin{cases} 5\,\text{ns} & \text{if } \tilde{s} = \text{calc} \\ 0\,\text{ns} & \text{if } \tilde{s} = \text{out} \\ \infty & \text{otherwise.} \end{cases}
\end{aligned}
$$

Figure 2.3 depicts the trajectories of the model for some input events. 5 ns after the first input event with the value 6 is received, an output event with value 4 is emitted. Please note that the given model M discards input events if another input event is received within the output value calculation duration, i.e. state s = calc. This case is demonstrated by the second and third input events with values 1 and 2 in Figure 2.3. This behaviour is due to the encoding of the δ_{int} function. The receipt of the third input event changes the state from $("calc", 1)$ to $\delta_{int}(("calc", 1), 2, e) = ("calc", 2)$ for $0\,ns < e < 5\,ns$.

2.2 Synthesizable DEVS

The original DEVS formalism has some downsides in regard to automatic hardware or software synthesis of models. These downsides are event bags for events, port couplings with multiple sources, inexplicit specified output behaviour of confluent transitions, and disallow of port back couplings. Therefore, the SynDEVS formalism is introduced defeating these weaknesses of the original formalism. Its main goal is to preserve as much as possible of the original DEVS expressiveness without loosing the capability of synthesis. Before representing a formal definition of SynDEVS the downsides of original DEVS are discussed in detail in the next subsections. Then, SynDEVS is introduced including some additional features, i.e. component variables, port/variable/conditional expressions, and a graphical representation of atomic components.

2.2.1 Output Port Event Bags

The introduction of event bags within original DEVS is one of the main issues which impede the synthesis of models into hardware or software. It is possible at atomic components to emit an arbitrary (possibly infinite) amount of events over a single output port within a single point in time. Therefore, all emitted events for the same source (i.e. an output port) are collected in a bag, i.e. a multiset[1]. Representing such a bag in hard- or software would require a possibly infinite amount of memory resources to store all emitted events. Occasionally, this behaviour is not synthesizable. The following atomic component M_∞ depicts such a computable but non-synthesizable DEVS model which outputs a recursively enumerable set of

---

[1] In mathematics, a multiset (or bag) is a generalization of a set where multiple instances of the same member may appear in the set. Other proposed names for multisets are listed in [Knu98, pp. 694].

Figure 2.4 Trajectories for the example atomic DEVS model M_∞. Output events are shown in relation to the model state. The output behaviour is computable but not synthesizable as it emits an unbound count of events.

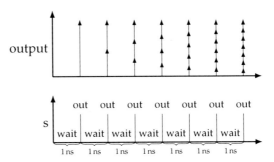

events.

$$M_\infty = (P_{in}, P_{out}, X, Y, S, s_0, \delta_{int}, \delta_{ext}, \delta_{con}, \lambda, \tau)$$

where

$$P_{in} = \varnothing$$
$$P_{out} = \{\text{"output"}\}$$
$$X = \varnothing$$
$$P_{out,output} = 1$$
$$S = \{\text{wait}, \text{out}\} \times \mathbb{N} \times \mathbb{N}$$
$$s_0 = (\text{wait}, 1, 1)$$
$$\delta_{int}((\tilde{s}, n, m)) = \begin{cases} (\text{out}, n, 1) & \text{if } \tilde{s} = \text{wait} \\ (\text{out}, n, m+1) & \text{if } \tilde{s} = \text{out} \wedge m < n \\ (\text{wait}, n+1, 1) & \text{otherwise} \end{cases}$$
$$\delta_{ext}(s, x, e) = s_0$$
$$\delta_{con}(s, x, e) = s_0$$
$$\lambda((\text{out}, n, m)) = 1$$
$$\tau((\tilde{s}, n, m)) = \begin{cases} 1\,\text{ns} & \text{if } \tilde{s} = \text{wait} \\ 0\,\text{ns} & \text{otherwise.} \end{cases}$$

Figure 2.4 depicts the output event count in relation to the state of the model. M_∞ toggles between the "wait" and "out" state. The "out" state outputs within a single point in time up to $n \in \mathbb{N}$ events. The "wait" state advances the time by 1 ns and increments the upper bound n by one each time. Taken together, the model M_∞ has a computable (i.e. n events after n ns) but non-synthesizable output behaviour. On the other hand,

DEVS models with infinite bag size (i.e. without an upper bound) are certainly impractical themselves. One could not even simulate the model behaviour: The simulation would not terminate as infinite events would have to be generated. Thus, it is sufficient to focus on DEVS models with a bounded output behaviour, i.e. models where an upper bound for the emitted event count within a single point in time exists. Such models can be easily transformed into equivalent DEVS models which only emit a single event over each output port within a single point in time. Before this model transformation is discussed in detail some definitions and theorems must be introduced to understand the model transformation.

Definition 1 (δ_{int} reachable). Let $\{s_0, \ldots, s_n\} = \tilde{S} \subseteq S$ be a subset of an atomic component's states S; then the state s_n is called δ_{int} reachable in $\tilde{S}$ from s_0 if, and only if, a finite δ_{int} transition sequence exists with

$$s_1 = \delta_{int}(s_0)$$
$$s_2 = \delta_{int}(s_1) = \delta_{int}(\delta_{int}(s_0))$$
$$\vdots$$
$$s_n = \delta_{int}(s_{n-1}) = \underbrace{\delta_{int}(\delta_{int}(\ldots \delta_{int}(s_0)\ldots))}_{n \text{ times}}.$$

Definition 2 (δ_{con} reachable). Let $\{s_0, \ldots, s_n\} = \tilde{S} \subseteq S$ be a subset of an atomic component's states S; then the state s_n is called δ_{con} reachable in $\tilde{S}$ from s_0 if, and only if, a finite δ_{con} transition sequence exists with

$$s_1 = \delta_{con}(s_0)$$
$$s_2 = \delta_{con}(s_1) = \delta_{con}(\delta_{con}(s_0))$$
$$\vdots$$
$$s_n = \delta_{con}(s_{n-1}) = \underbrace{\delta_{con}(\delta_{con}(\ldots \delta_{con}(s_0)\ldots))}_{n \text{ times}}.$$

Definition 3 (Cycle free). Let $\{s_0, \ldots, s_n\} = \tilde{S} \subseteq S$ be a subset of an atomic component's states S where s_n is δ_{con} or δ_{int} reachable in $\tilde{S}$ from s_0; then this transition sequence is called *cycle free* if, and only if, each state $s_i \in \tilde{S}$ is not δ_{int} (or δ_{con}) reachable in S from itself.

Definition 4 (Zero-timeout chain). Let $\{s_0, \ldots, s_n\} = \tilde{S}_{zerotimeout} \subseteq S$ be a subset of an atomic component's states. Then, these states are called a *zero-timeout chain* if, and only if, the timeout for every state is zero (i.e. $\forall s_i \in \tilde{S}_{\text{zerotimeout}}.\tau(s_i) = 0$) and s_n is δ_{int} (or δ_{con}) reachable in $\tilde{S}_{\text{zerotimeout}}$ from s_0.

Theorem 1. *Within an atomic component the longest cycle free zero-timeout chain with length n determines the upper bound n of possible output events which may occur within a single point in time at each output port.*

Proof. Within original DEVS an output event may be emitted in two cases: (I) a timeout event occurred alone or (II), both, a timeout event and an external event occurred together. In both cases a state change is initiated and the successor state s' is determined either by the δ_{int} function, i.e. case (I), or the δ_{con} function, i.e. case (II). However, if we want to emit more then a single event within a single point in time we have to subsequently generate timeout events by setting the timeout of the state s' to $\tau(s') = 0$. Thus, the proof must be split up into two parts: Firstly, it must be proven that a zero-timeout chain with length n can emit n output events and secondly, it must be proven that this zero-timeout chain can emit n output events at the utmost.

Without loss of generality we may assume that there exists a longest cycle free zero-timeout chain of states $\{s_0, \ldots, s_n\} = \tilde{S}_{\text{zerotimeout}} \subseteq S$ with length n. Thus, each state $s_i \in \tilde{S}_{\text{zerotimeout}}$ within this chain may emit an output event *once* at each of the output ports. Taken together, after the atomic component entered this zero-timeout chain it may emit up to n events within a single point in time at each of the output ports.

Assume to the contrary that there may exist another cycle free zero-timeout chain which emit $n' > n$ events. Then, there must be another δ_{int} (or δ_{con}) transition within $\tilde{S}_{\text{zerotimeout}}$ which emit at least one additional output event. Such an additional transition could be a δ_{int} (or δ_{con}) transition (I) within two states from $\tilde{S}_{\text{zerotimeout}}$ or (II) from a state of $\tilde{S}_{\text{zerotimeout}}$ to a state in S. However, the first case conflicts with the cycle free property of the zero-timeout chain, contradicting our assumption. Case (II) would make this new cycle free zero-timeout chain longer than the original one, again contradicting our assumption.

Taken both parts together, a zero-timeout chain of length n may emit up to n output events and there may not exist another zero-timeout chain with the same length emitting more then n events. Thus, within an atomic component the longest cycle free zero-timeout chain with length n determines the upper bound n of possible output events which may occur within a single point in time at each output port. $\square$

Corollary 1. *An atomic component with a cyclic zero-timeout chain may emit infinite output events.*

This follows directly from a state s with an internal transition loop ($\delta_{int}(s) = s$) and zero-timeout $\tau(s) = 0$. Then, after the model enters this state s an infinite amount of output events could be generated.

The following atomic component M_n depicts a DEVS model with a cycle-free zero-timeout chain with upper bound of 3 for the zero-timeout chain length.

$$M_n = (P_{in}, P_{out}, X, Y, S, s_0, \delta_{int}, \delta_{ext}, \delta_{con}, \lambda, \tau)$$

where

$$
\begin{aligned}
P_{in} &= \varnothing \\
P_{out} &= \{\text{"output"}\} \\
X &= \varnothing \\
P_{out,output} &= 1 \\
S &= \{\text{wait, out}\} \times \mathbb{N} \times \mathbb{N} \\
s_0 &= (\text{wait}, 1, 1) \\
\delta_{int}\left((\tilde{s}, n, m)\right) &=
\begin{cases}
(\text{out}, n, 1) & \text{if } \tilde{s} = \text{wait} \\
(\text{out}, n, m+1) & \text{if } \tilde{s} = \text{out} \wedge m < n \\
(\text{wait}, n, 1) & \text{if } \tilde{s} = \text{out} \wedge m = 3 \\
(\text{wait}, n+1, 1) & \text{otherwise}
\end{cases} \\
\delta_{ext}\left(s, x, e\right) &= s_0 \\
\delta_{con}(s, x, e) &= s_0 \\
\lambda\left((\text{out}, n, m)\right) &= 1 \\
\tau\left((\tilde{s}, n, m)\right) &=
\begin{cases}
1\,\text{ns} & \text{if } \tilde{s} = \text{wait} \\
0\,\text{ns} & \text{otherwise.}
\end{cases}
\end{aligned}
$$

Basically, it is constructed in the same way like the previous atomic component M_∞ but, in contrast, the count of the zero-timeout states ("out", n, m) is limited. Instead of allowing the chain to increase by one after each execution of the complete chain, i.e.

$$(\text{"wait"}, n, 1) \xrightarrow{\delta_{int}} \underbrace{(\text{"out"}, n, 0) \xrightarrow{\delta_{int}} \ldots \xrightarrow{\delta_{int}} (\text{"out"}, n, n)}_{n+1 \text{ zero-timeout states (\text{"out"}}, n, \ldots)} \xrightarrow{\delta_{int}} (\text{"wait"}, n+1, 1)$$

Figure 2.5 Trajectories
for the example atomic
DEVS model M_n. Output
events are shown in re-
lation to the model state.
The output behaviour is
computable and possibly
synthesizable.

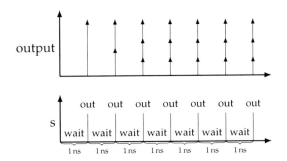

the length is bounded to an upper limit of three, i.e. for $n = 3$ it is

$$("wait", n, 1) \xrightarrow{\delta_{int}} \underbrace{("out", n, 1) \xrightarrow{\delta_{int}} \ldots \xrightarrow{\delta_{int}} ("out", n, n)}_{n = 3 \text{ zero-timeout states } ("out", n, \ldots)} \xrightarrow{\delta_{int}} ("wait", n, 1).$$

Figure 2.5 depicts the output event count in relation to the state of the
model. As the output event count is bounded to a finite number of emitted
events it is synthesizable: An finite upper bound for the output port's
event bag exists and, additionally, this upper bound is computable. Please
note that without giving further implementation details of such an abstract
event bag, it is still possible to conclude that an implementation of the event
bag is possible due to its limited resource usage, i.e. its finite upper bound
of events to store. However, by introducing some simple transformation
rules, it is possible to completely eliminate the use of event bags.

The goal of the transformation is that within a zero-timeout chain the
modified model emits only a single output event over each output port at
the utmost. Therefore, the following transformations must be applied to
the model:

1. Identify all output ports $p_i \in P_{bagout} \subseteq P_{out}$ within zero-timeout chains
   which emits multiple output events.

2. Calculate the overall maximum output event count n for all those output
   ports p_i. Please note that such an upper limit exists, recall Theorem 1.
   Without loss of generality we may assume that n is the length of the
   longest zero-timeout chain.

3. For each port p_i create indexed copies p_i^j for $j = 1, \ldots, n$. Each new port
   will be used to emit a single output event within the zero-timeout chain.

4. Replace at the j-th state s_j of each zero-timeout chain the use of port p_i to port p_i^j. Thus, a new output function λ' is created in which the use of the output ports p_i is partially substituted with the new ports p_i^j, i.e.

$$
\begin{aligned}
\lambda'_p(s) &= \lambda_p(s) &&\text{for all } p \notin P_{\text{bagout}} \\
\lambda'_{p_i}(s) &= \diamond &&\text{for all } p_i \in P_{\text{bagout}} \\
\lambda'_{p_i^j}(s_j) &= \lambda_{p_i}(s_j) &&\text{for each } j\text{-th state } s_j \text{ of the zero-timeout chains.}
\end{aligned}
$$

Please note that $\diamond$ means the absent event, i.e. no event is emitted or received over the output or input port.

Taken together, the new output function preserve the original output function behaviour except that the multiple event outputs of the ports p_i are replaced by single event outputs of the ports p_i^j in each j-th state s_j of the zero-timeout chains. However, these transformation renders the models structural incompatible to the receiving components. Thus, the receiver has to be transformed equivalent regarding its input ports (i.e. introduce n input ports and rewrite transition conditions and assignments accordingly).

The concept of denoting the absence of an event with a special value or symbol is a common method within synchronous and timed models of computation, cf. [Jan04]. By introducing an absent event symbol to denote the absence of an event at a specific point in time within a signal, the causality and continuity of events are maintained [LSV98]. Even more, the signals events implicitly carry the timing information with them to denote when they appeared. Thus, global time is elegantly represented and distributed within. Other popular approaches to handle timing within a MoC are to tag each event with timing information (time-tag approach) or to introduce local timers at each MoCs process which itself have access to some globally distributed time (local-timer approach) [Jan04]. These approaches are exploited by the δ-delay model used in popular hardware description languages such as VHDL [Vhd87], Verilog [Ver96], or SystemC [Sys06].

Example

The following atomic DEVS model M_n' exemplifies the transformation for the atomic DEVS model M_n. Figure 2.6 depicts the trajectories of the transformed model. Each output port emits a single event within the zero-timeout chain only.

Figure 2.6 Trajectories for the transformed atomic DEVS model M'_n of M_n. Output events are shown in relation to the model state. No event bags are necessary as a single event is emitted at each output port only.

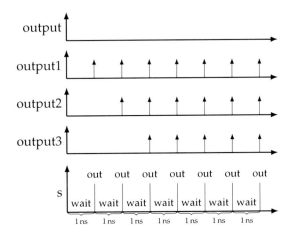

$$M'_n = (P_{\text{in}}, P_{\text{out}}, X, Y, S, s_0, \delta_{\text{int}}, \delta_{\text{ext}}, \delta_{\text{con}}, \lambda, \tau)$$

where

$$
\begin{aligned}
P_{\text{in}} &= \varnothing \\
P_{\text{out}} &= \{\text{"output"}, \text{"output1"}, \text{"output2"}, \text{"output3"}\} \\
X &= \varnothing \\
P_{\text{out,output}} &= 1 \\
P_{\text{out,output1}} &= 1 \\
P_{\text{out,output2}} &= 1 \\
P_{\text{out,output3}} &= 1 \\
S &= \{\text{wait, out}\} \times \mathbb{N} \times \mathbb{N} \\
s_0 &= (\text{wait}, 1, 1)
\end{aligned}
$$

$$
\delta_{\text{int}}((\tilde{s}, n, m)) =
\begin{cases}
(\text{out}, n, 1) & \text{if } \tilde{s} = \text{wait} \\
(\text{out}, n, m+1) & \text{if } \tilde{s} = \text{out} \wedge m < n \\
(\text{wait}, n, 1) & \text{if } \tilde{s} = \text{out} \wedge m = 3 \\
(\text{wait}, n+1, 1) & \text{otherwise}
\end{cases}
$$

$$
\begin{aligned}
\delta_{\text{ext}}(s, x, e) &= s_0 \\
\delta_{\text{con}}(s, x, e) &= s_0 \\
\lambda_{\text{output}}((\text{out}, n, m)) &= \diamond \\
\lambda_{\text{output1}}((\text{out}, n, 1)) &= 1 \\
\lambda_{\text{output2}}((\text{out}, n, 2)) &= 1
\end{aligned}
$$

$$\lambda_{\text{output3}}\left((\text{out}, n, 3)\right) \ = \ 1$$

$$\tau\left((\tilde{s}, n, m)\right) \ = \ \begin{cases} 1\,\text{ns} & \text{if } \tilde{s} = \text{wait} \\ 0\,\text{ns} & \text{otherwise.} \end{cases}$$

2.2.2 Confluent Transition Function Output Behaviour

The introduction of the confluent transition function δ_{con} within the original DEVS formalism (i.e. Parallel DEVS) in [ZKP00] did not define adequately enough the output behaviour of it. It is undefined whether the output is directly related to the (possibly multiple) use of δ_{int} within δ_{con} or only to δ_{con}. In the first case, the multiple use of δ_{int} within δ_{con} would lead to multiple output events (i.e. a single output event for each δ_{int} occurrence). Contrary in the second case, only a single output event would be emitted.

Theorem 2. *An atomic component entering the state $s \in S$ will emit the output $\lambda(s)$ if and only if a timeout event occur (i.e. no input event occurred until the timeout value $e = \tau(s)$ is hit).*

Proof. The output behaviour of DEVS models is weakly defined in such a way that an output event is emitted when an internal transition is executed. An internal transition and, thus, an output event, occur if and only if the timeout event $e = \tau(s)$ occur. The next state of the models is computed either by $\delta_{\text{int}}(s)$ alone (case 1) or by possibly multiple occurrences of δ_{int} within $\delta_{\text{con}}(s)$ (case 2) if an input event is received at the timeout.

Case 1 is trivial as the single use of δ_{int} only allows a single output. Thus, the output is well defined.

Case 2 could lead to multiple output events as multiple δ_{int} transitions could be used within $\delta_{\text{con}}(s)$. Theorem 2 does not allow this behaviour. However, this is no restriction as an equivalent model can be generated in terms of output behaviour. Consider the following model with multiple outputs within a single δ_{con} transition:

$$\delta_{\text{int}}(s_1) \ = \ s_2$$
$$\delta_{\text{int}}(s_2) \ = \ s_3$$
$$\delta_{\text{con}}(s_1) \ = \ \underbrace{\delta_{\text{int}}(\delta_{\text{int}}(s_1))}_{\lambda(s_1)} = \underbrace{\delta_{\text{int}}(s_2)}_{\lambda(s_2)} = s_3$$

The next state will be determined by $\delta_{con}(s_1)$ if the model is in state s_1 and an input event occur together with the timeout $e = \tau(s_1)$. As δ_{con} make use of of two internal transitions (i.e. $\delta_{int}(s_1)$ and $\delta_{int}(s_2)$) two output events (i.e. $\lambda(s_1)$ and $\lambda(s_2)$) will be emitted. Even if the original DEVS semantics would allow such a behaviour it is not allowed in terms of Theorem 2. However, an equivalent model can be generated with the same output behaviour. The basic concept of this model transformation is to introduce a set of help states with zero timeout $\tau(s) = 0$ generating the required output events. Consider the help states $s_1', s_2' \in S$ with $\tau(s_1') = \tau(s_2') = 0$:

$$
\begin{aligned}
\delta_{int}(s_1) &= s_2 \\
\delta_{int}(s_1') &= s_2' \\
\delta_{int}(s_2) &= s_3 \\
\delta_{int}(s_2') &= s_3 \\
\delta_{con}(s_1) &= s_1'
\end{aligned}
$$

The model output behaviour is equivalent but without violating Theorem 2. The $\delta_{con}(s_1)$ transition now enters the helper states s_1' and s_2' which themselves then generate the required outputs $\lambda(s_1') = \lambda(s_1)$ and $\lambda(s_2') = \lambda(s_2)$ within the same point in time. Taken together, Theorem 2 is not a restriction of the models output behaviour because an equivalent model can be generated in terms of output behaviour. Thus, it details the DEVS semantics more clearly.   □

2.2.3 Component Interconnection

Input and output ports may be coupled together without almost any restrictions within the original DEVS as detailed in Section 2.1.1. The only constraint is that a connection between an input port and an output port of the same component (i.e. a direct feedback loop) is not allowed. However, multiple output ports may be connected to a single input port. Thus, multiple driver may exist for the same sink. All output ports may emit events within a single port in time and, in doing so, all incoming events at the input port are collected in an event bag. Figure 2.7 depicts such a situation. The output port of components $A_1, \ldots, A_n$ are connected all to the same input port of component B. Thus, this input port has multiple drivers and may receive multiple events within the same point in time which have to be collected in an event bag.

Figure 2.7 Multiple output ports driving a single input port. Incoming events are collected within an input port event bag.

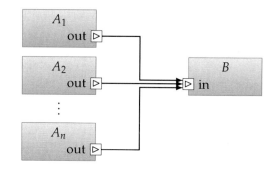

Input port event bags can be eliminated likewise the output port event bags from Section 2.2.1 by port replication. Basically, every input port with multiple drivers is replicated and then directly connected to a single driver until the original input port has only a single driver left. In detail, the following transformations have to be applied to the model to eliminate the input port event bags:

1. Identify all ports with multiple drivers. These are either the inner components input ports P_{in} or the toplevel parallel component's output ports. For each input port count the number of connections. Multiple drivers are connected to this sink if the connection count is greater than one.

2. Let n be the connection count of the port p with multiple drivers. Rename the port p to p_1 and create $n - 1$ copies $p_2, \ldots, p_n$ of port p_1.

3. Enumerate all original connections to port p. Then, for the i-th connection with $i = 1, \ldots, n$ reconnect the connection to the numbered copy p_i of input port p.

4. Rewrite the components behaviour (i.e. transition condition and assignments) to handle the new ports.

Please note that the presented transformation does not change the overall behaviour of the model. Only its inner structure in terms of input and output port and their connections is changed. Even more, modified models in terms of the described port replications from Section 2.2.1 or Section 2.2.3 may be seamlessly embedded into original DEVS, which is detailed in the latter.

The following DEVS model illustrate how to embed a SynDEVS model back into an original DEVS model (i.e. one with input port bags). Basically,

Figure 2.8 The model
from Figure 2.7 after the
applied transformation.
The input event bag for
port in of component B
is eliminated. Annotated
to the connections are
the enumeration numbers
from the transformation
algorithm.

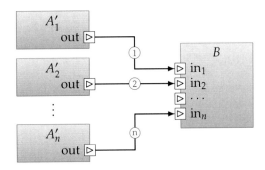

a parent parallel component is created including the transformed components $A'_1, A'_2, \ldots,$ and A'_n. Additionally, an atomic component acting as an
event bridge interface reconstructing the original input event behaviour of
component B is added, cf. Figure 2.9.

The parallel component N is

$$N_{bridge} = (P_{in}, P_{out}, X, Y, M, C_{in}, C_{out}, C_{inner})$$

where

$$P_{in} = \{\}$$
$$P_{out} = \{"out"\}$$
$$X = \varnothing$$
$$P_{out,out} = \bigcup_{i=1}^{n} P_{out,out} \text{ of } A'_i$$
$$M = \left\{(a'_{bridge}, A'_{bridge})\right\} \cup \bigcup_{i=1}^{n} \left\{(a'_i, A'_i)\right\}$$
$$C_{in} = \varnothing$$
$$C_{out} = \left\{\left((a'_{bridge}, out), (N_{bridge}, out)\right)\right\}$$
$$C_{inner} = \bigcup_{i=1}^{n} \left\{\left((a'_i, out), (a'_{bridge}, in_i)\right)\right\}.$$

The embedded atomic component A'_{bridge} acting as a bridge in-between
the SynDEVS and original DEVS is

$$A'_{bridge} = (P_{in}, P_{out}, X, Y, S, s_0, \delta_{int}, \delta_{ext}, \delta_{con}, \lambda, \tau)$$

Figure 2.9 A model including a bridging interface atomic component A'_{bridge} to embedded SynDEVS components into original DEVS models, reassembling its input port event bag behaviour.

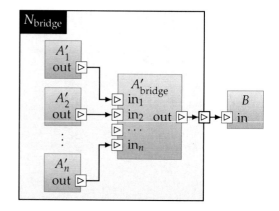

where

$$P_{in} = \bigcup_{i=1}^{n} \{"in_i"\}$$

$$P_{out} = \{"out"\}$$

$$P_{in,in_i} = P_{out,out} \text{ of } A'_i \qquad \text{for } i = 1,\ldots,n$$

$$P_{out,out} = \bigcup_{i=1}^{n} P_{out,out} \text{ of } A'_i$$

$$S = \{wait, out\} \times B \qquad (B \text{ is a bag/multiset})$$

$$s_0 = (wait, \varnothing)$$

$$\delta_{int}\left((\tilde{s}, B)\right) = s_0$$

$$\delta_{ext}\left((\tilde{s}, B), x, e\right) = \left(out, \bigcup_{i=1}^{n} x_{in_i}\right)$$

$$\delta_{con}(s, x, e) = \delta_{ext}\left(\delta_{int}(s), x, e\right)$$

$$\lambda\left((out, B)\right) = B$$

$$\tau\left((\tilde{s}, B)\right) = \begin{cases} 0\,ns & \text{if } \tilde{s} = out \\ \infty & \text{otherwise.} \end{cases}$$

The bridge toggles between the wait and out states. The wait state initialize an empty output event bag B. Whenever an event occur at one of its input puts, possibly together with other events at the other input ports,

the external transition is executed. Then, the all incoming events are collected into the bag and, afterwards, directly output at the output port by
the out state. Thus, the single events are reassembled and transmitted to
the receivers input port bag reconstructing the original behaviour.

Finally, after showing that event bags at ports and multiple port drivers
can be eliminated in terms of a transformation into a behaviour equivalent
model, SynDEVS is now formally defined.

2.2.4 Parallel Components

A parallel component is defined of the same structure like the original
DEVS parallel component by an 8-tuple

$$\text{SynDEVS}_{\text{parallel}} = (P_{\text{in}}, P_{\text{out}}, X, Y, M, C_{\text{in}}, C_{\text{out}}, C_{\text{inner}})$$

with

$$
\begin{aligned}
P_{\text{in}} &= \text{input ports} \\
P_{\text{out}} &= \text{output ports} \\
X &= \text{event values for each input port} \\
Y &= \text{event values for each output port} \\
M &= \text{inner atomic or parallel components} \\
C_{\text{in}} &= \text{connections between input ports and inner components} \\
C_{\text{out}} &= \text{connections between inner components and output ports} \\
C_{\text{inner}} &= \text{connections in-between inner components.}
\end{aligned}
$$

The same rules and constraints from the original DEVS parallel component apply. However, to defeat the multiple port drivers, an additional
constraint regarding the port couplings must be introduced. Thus, each
port shall only have a single driver, which splits into two different rules:

1. Inner atomic or parallel components input ports may only have a single
   inner atomic or parallel component output port or a single toplevel

parallel component input port connected to them, i.e.

$$\forall \left((c_{\text{source}}, p_{\text{source}}), (c_{\text{sink}}, p_{\text{sink}}) \right) \in C_{\text{in}} \cup C_{\text{inner}} \Rightarrow$$
$$\neg \exists \left((c'_{\text{source}}, p_{\text{source}}), (c_{\text{sink}}, p_{\text{sink}}) \right) \in C_{\text{in}} \cup C_{\text{inner}}.$$
$$(c_{\text{source}}, p_{\text{source}}) = (c'_{\text{source}}, p_{\text{source}}).$$

2. The toplevel parallel component output ports may only have have a single inner atomic or parallel component output port or a single toplevel parallel component input port connected to them[2], i.e.

$$\forall \left((c_{\text{source}}, p_{\text{source}}), (c_{\text{sink}}, p_{\text{sink}}) \right) \in C_{\text{out}} \Rightarrow$$
$$\neg \exists \left((c'_{\text{source}}, p_{\text{source}}), (c_{\text{sink}}, p_{\text{sink}}) \right) \in C_{\text{out}}.$$
$$(c_{\text{source}}, p_{\text{source}}) = (c'_{\text{source}}, p_{\text{source}}).$$

2.2.5 Atomic Components

An atomic component within SynDEVS is almost the same like an atomic component of the original DEVS formalism. However, some changes are introduced for making the SynDEVS models synthesizable. In addition, the structure and behaviour of atomic components are specified more formal than in the original DEVS formalism to define the execution semantic unambiguously.

An SynDEVS atomic component is denoted by an 15-tuple

$$\text{SynDEVS}_{\text{atomic}} = (P_{\text{in}}, P_{\text{out}}, X, Y, V, W, v_{\text{init}}, v, S, s_0, \delta_{\text{int}}, \delta_{\text{ext}}, \delta_{\text{con}}, \lambda, \tau)$$

with

$$
\begin{aligned}
P_{\text{in}} &= \text{input ports} \\
P_{\text{out}} &= \text{output ports} \\
X &= \text{event values for each input port} \\
Y &= \text{event values for each output port} \\
V &= \text{variables} \\
W &= \text{values for each variable} \\
v_{\text{init}} &= \text{initial values for each values}
\end{aligned}
$$

---

[2] Please note that a toplevel parallel component output port may not be directly coupled to one of the component's input ports by definition, cf. C_{out}, C_{out}, and C_{inner} at Section 2.1.1.

$$\begin{aligned}
v &= \text{variable assignment functions} \\
S &= \text{non-empty set of state names} \\
s_0 &= \text{start state} \\
\delta_{int} &= \text{internal transition function} \\
\delta_{ext} &= \text{external transition function} \\
\delta_{con} &= \text{confluent transition function} \\
\lambda &= \text{output function} \\
\tau &= \text{timeout function.}
\end{aligned}$$

Input and Output Ports

An atomic component has a finite set of port names P which must not be explicitly defined. The port names set is a result from the disjunct split of the ports into input and output port names. Both, input ports P_{in} and output ports P_{out} are defined as a tuple of port names

$$\begin{aligned}
P_{in} &= (p_1, \ldots, p_n) \quad \text{with } p_i \in P \text{ and} \\
P_{out} &= (p'_1, \ldots, p'_m) \quad \text{with } p'_i \in P.
\end{aligned}$$

To easily access the different ports they may be referenced directly by their name (e.g. $P_{in,clk}$ for the input port named "clk") or by their tuple index value (e.g. $P_{out,2}$ for the 2nd port in P_{out}). In addition, the output and input ports have to be disjunct (i.e. no port should be both an input and an output port) which is the condition

$$\bigcup_{i=1}^{n} \{P_{in,i}\} \cap \bigcup_{j=1}^{m} \{P_{out,j}\} = \emptyset$$

and no port name may be used more than once, i.e. $m + n = |P|$.

Each input and output port has an associated finite set of event values. To indicate the absence of an event at a port, the additional symbol $\diamond$ is added to the ports finite set of event values.

$$\begin{aligned}
X_i &= V \cup \{\diamond\} \quad \text{with an arbitrary set of values } V \text{ for input port } P_{in,i} \text{ and} \\
Y_j &= V \cup \{\diamond\} \quad \text{with an arbitrary set of values } V \text{ for output port } P_{out,j}.
\end{aligned}$$

Additionally, the complete input event value set X and output event value set Y are defined as a set of sets with

$$X = X_1 \times X_2 \times \ldots X_n \quad \text{and} \quad Y = Y_1 \times Y_2 \times \cdots \times Y_n.$$

Variables

Temporary data within original DEVS has to be stored in the model in terms of encoding the data into state space. Usually, the state set S is a product of an explicit state set and state related data sets (e.g. counters, temporary values, ...). However, this state encoding make the DEVS models behaviour hard to understand in terms of readability. Therefore, variables were introduced within SynDEVS.

Like the ports definition, a finite set of variable names may be defined with a tuple $V = (v_1, \ldots, v_n)$ within a SynDEVS atomic component. Likewise, the variables may be accessed by their index position within the tuple (e.g. v_3 for the third variable in V) or directly by their variable name (e.g. v_{count} for the variable named "count"). For each variable a set of possible variable values must be defined by

$$W_i = T \cup \{\diamond\} \quad \text{with an arbitrary value set } T \text{ for variable } v_i.$$

The set of sets $W = W_1 \times \ldots W_n$ is describing all possible values of the variables and, thus, the models variables state is a member of W.

Within original DEVS, a state transition by δ_{int}, δ_{ext}, or δ_{con} may change embedded variables of S explicitly by their target state. However, in SynDEVS the variables may be only changed in terms of entering a state. Thus, states, variables, and output functions can be seen as a representation of a combinatorial calculation feed into a register. By entering a state the calculation is started comparable to a change of input values of a combinatorial circuit. Then, the calculation is done in terms of variable assignments which is represented by the values wandering through the combinatorial circuit. Afterwards, the calculation is finished and the calculated value can be emitted in terms of the output function which is like the refreshing of the value stored in the register at the end a clocked combinatorial circuit. Please note that this should not imply that SynDEVS atomic components can be seen on the same abstraction level as registers and combinatorial circuits. Such a comparison helps to portrait how state entering, variable assignment, and output events are correlated.

The initial variable values are defined by the tuple $v_{\text{init}} = (w_1, \ldots, w_n)$ with $w_i \in W_i$. For each variable $v_i \in V$ a function $v_i : S \times X \times W \to W_i$

Figure 2.10 Relation of state and variable changes in SynDEVS atomic components

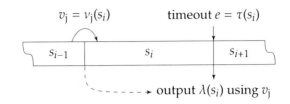

$v_j = v_j(s_i)$ ⠀⠀⠀⠀ timeout $e = \tau(s_i)$

s_{i-1} ⠀⠀ s_i ⠀⠀ s_{i+1}

output $\lambda(s_i)$ using v_j

must be defined. Whenever a state is changed in terms of δ_{int}, δ_{ext}, or δ_{con} then the function v_j is evaluated for the target state and the variable values are changed accordingly. Figure 2.10 depicts this behaviour. The variable v_j is changed in terms of the state change to s_i by the evaluation of $v_j = v_j(s_i, x_1, \ldots, x_n, v_1, \ldots v_n)$. The set $X = \{x_1, \ldots, x_n\}$ of the assignment function preimages are the current input port values. These values are either the last received event value or $\diamond$ if no value was received before.

If a variable value should not be changed, the assignment function must evaluate to the value $\diamond \in W_i$. Thus, the variable assignment functions are total and the function space $v = v_1 \times \cdots \times v_n$ describes the assignments for all variables and all states.

Variables may be used within other variable computations, transition conditions, or output functions. If they are used within variable assignment functions, which take place when entering a state, the variable values are *concurrently* assigned (i.e. all new values of the variables are first computed and, afterwards, assigned all together, see [Dij76, pp. 28]). Otherwise, variables used within output functions or as transition conditions, which are evaluated when leaving the state, are exploited by their newly assigned value.

The introduction of variables highly increases the readability of the model. Additionally, for the visual programming paradigm introduced later on in Section 2.4, it would not be possible for the designer to include variable data within the state space. Within the graphical representation of SynDEVS atomic components, the state space is purely a set of descriptive names nor any other kind of data. Thus, variables are necessary to not reduce the expressiveness in terms of model behaviour compared to atomic components of the original DEVS formalism.

Theorem 3. *Temporary values may be stored within the state space set implicitly (e.g. original DEVS) or with a dedicated set of variables explicitly (e.g. SynDEVS). Both representations are equivalent in terms of expressiveness of the model.*

Proof. Let S be a state set of the original DEVS formalism in such a way that it is a product of names describing the model's state and a finite count of temporary variable sets V_i (i.e. $S = \{$set of state names$\} \times W_1 \times \cdots \times W_n$). The state space is exploited within the transition functions δ_{int}, δ_{ext}, and δ_{con}, the output function λ, and the timeout function τ. The model's current state is read within all of those functions and written by each function except the timeout function.

Showing the equivalence of implicit and explicit variable declarations can be done with the help of an intermediate variable declaration in terms of variables which are written during transition execution and not by state entry. Instead of storing the variables data within the state space (e.g. $S = \{$set of state names$\times W_1 \times \cdots \times W_n)$, the variables $V_1, \ldots, V_n$ are store explicit in their own sets and the state space S are the state names solely. Then, the preimage and image of the functions using the variables have to be modified to include the explicitly defined variables (e.g. $\delta_{int}(S \times W_1 \times \cdots \times W_n) \rightarrow (S \times W_1 \times \cdots \times W_n)$). Even more, the variables may be written with the help of dedicated functions (i.e. introduce new variable writing functions $v_{int,i}$, $v_{ext,i}$ and $v_{con,i}$) resulting in a partition of functions defining the next state (i.e. δ_{int}, δ_{ext}, and δ_{con}) and the next value of the variables (i.e. $v_{int,i}$, $v_{ext,i}$, and $v_{con,i}$). Thus, only the transition functions preimage has to be modified to include the variables. Whenever the atomic component change its state the state transition functions are evaluated in parallel to the variable writing functions. Clearly, regardless of which type of writing a variable is used, the expressiveness stays the same and both approaches are equal.

The splitting of the variables' assignments into their own functions has a great impact on the readability of the model. Within original DEVS, just by looking at the state transition functions and the embedded writing of variables a chain of causation is implied. When a transition occur the transition function is evaluated for the current state and the result defines, both, the next state as well as the new variable values. Thus, the implied causality is that, firstly, the transition function is evaluated resulting in the following state of the model and, secondly, new values are concurrently assigned to the variables after the new state is entered. Contrary, this chain of causation is invalid after introducing the variable assignment functions. For instance, a model is in state s_i and the timeout event occur, resulting in an internal transition to state s_{i+1}. However, setting the variables new values are not done by the evaluation of $v_{int,i}$ for the target state s_{i+1}, instead it is evaluated for the old state s_i. Even more complicated, from a target state's perspective it must be evaluated which incoming transition (i.e. internal, external, or confluent) led to the current state. Thus, variable assignments are ambiguous and hard to read within the model's definition. Therefore, variables within SynDEVS are written when entering a state, and, thus, the readability of the model is increased in terms of unambiguous variable assignment behaviour.

One could argue that entering a state over different transitions can only lead to one type of variable assignment (i.e. v_i instead of one of $v_{int,i}$, $v_{ext,i}$, or $v_{con,i}$). However, this is not a reduction of the models expressiveness in terms of input and output behaviour as the original model may be transformed into a SynDEVS version with equivalent behaviour. It is related to the transformation of a Mealy to a Moore finite state machine as described in [MC07, pp. 86]. Along the different transformation paths additional zero-timeout states are introduced in between the source and target states of the transitions. Then, at each of these zero-timeout states the variable assignment function may replicate the original assignment behaviour. For instance, within an external transition from s_i to s_{i+1} an additional zero-timeout state $s_{i,ext}$ is introduced and the external transition is relinked to this state and the variable assignment functions are set to $v_i(s_{i,ext}) = v_{ext,i}(s_{i+1})$. After the transformation, the input and output behaviour of the resulting SynDEVS model is equivalent to the original model.

Taken all together, temporary values which are stored implicitly in the original DEVS state space may be equivalently stored explicitly by introducing variable spaces and assignment functions in terms of state entry. □

States and Transitions

The states, state timeout values, and the state transitions are encoded by

$$
\begin{aligned}
S &= \text{a non-empty set of state names (i.e. } \emptyset \subset S) \\
s_0 \in S &= \text{initial state } s_0 \text{ of the atomic component} \\
\tau : S \to \mathbb{R}^+ &= \text{timeout value for each state} \\
\delta_{int} : S \times W \to S &= \text{internal transition function} \\
\delta_{ext} : S \times X \times W \to S &= \text{external transition function} \\
\delta_{con} : S \times X \times W \to S &= \text{confluent transition function.}
\end{aligned}
$$

The transition functions behaviour within SynDEVS is likewise the behaviour of the functions within original DEVS. Thus, the δ_{int} transition function is used if the timeout of the current state occurred and each input ports value is $\diamond$ (i.e. no input events were received). If an input value at a port is received before the timeout occurred, the δ_{ext} transition function is exploited. However, if an input value is received while the timeout occurred, the δ_{con} transition function is used to calculate the next state of the model. Whenever a timeout event within an atomic component occur, the component may emit output events.

In contrast to transition, output, and variable assignment functions, the preimage of the timeout function τ does not include the variables. Thus, the timeout function is a pure constant function, which is necessary for automatically calculate the smallest step of time within the model as detailed later in Section 4.2.2.

Output Events

The output events are encoded by the output function $\lambda : S \times W \to Y$. In contrast to the original DEVS output behaviour, only the last event written to an output port within a zero-timeout chain is emitted.

Without loss of generality let assume that $s_1, \ldots, s_n \in S$ is a zero-timeout chain with $\delta_{int}(s_i) = s_{i+1}$ for $i = 1, \ldots, n-1$. During the δ_{int} or δ_{con} transitions in every intermediate state s_i with $i = 1, \ldots, n$ the output function $\lambda(s_i)$ is evaluated. If an output value is written to an output port, it is noted at the port but not yet emitted. In contrast, if the absent event $\diamond$ is written to an output port, no value should be emitted but a pending output event is not be removed. After the evaluation of the final state s_n output function $\lambda(s_n)$, all pending output events (i.e. up to one per output port) are emitted.

However, if multiple events should be emitted over the same port within a zero-timeout chain, one has to transform the model appropriately, cf. Section 2.2.1.

Example

SynDEVS atomic models ease the modelling of components with variables. In the following, an example model of a *ping pong* generator is presented which emits every 100 ns values from 1 to 5 and, afterwards, back down to 1 and so on and so forth. The ping pong generator is an atomic SynDEVS component

$$M_{pingpong} = (P_{in}, P_{out}, X, Y, V, W, v_{init}, v, S, s_0, \delta_{int}, \delta_{ext}, \delta_{con}, \lambda, \tau)$$

with

$$P_{in} \quad = \quad \varnothing$$

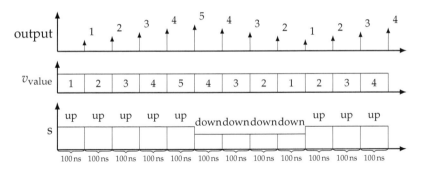

Figure 2.11 Trajectories for the atomic SynDEVS component M_{pingpong}.

$$
\begin{aligned}
P_{\text{out}} &= \{\text{"output"}\} \\
X &= \varnothing \\
Y_{\text{output}} &= \{1, \ldots, 5, \diamond\} \\
V &= \{\text{"value"}\} \\
W_{\text{value}} &= Y_{\text{output}} \\
v_{\text{init}} &= 1 \\
\nu_{\text{value}}(s, v_{\text{value}}) &= \begin{cases} v_{\text{value}} + 1 & \text{if } s = \text{up} \\ v_{\text{value}} - 1 & \text{if } s = \text{down} \end{cases} \\
S &= \{\text{up}, \text{down}\} \\
s_0 &= \text{up} \\
\delta_{\text{int}}(s, v_{\text{value}}) &= \begin{cases} \text{down} & \text{if } s = \text{up} \wedge v_{\text{value}} = 5 \\ \text{up} & \text{if } s = \text{down} \wedge v_{\text{value}} = 1 \\ s & \text{otherwise} \end{cases} \\
\delta_{\text{ext}}(s, x, v_{\text{value}}) &= \delta_{\text{con}}(s, x, v_{\text{value}}) = s_0 \\
\lambda_{\text{output}}(s, v_{\text{value}}) &= v_{\text{value}} \\
\tau(s) &= 100 \, \text{ns.}
\end{aligned}
$$

2.3 Reconfiguration

In [MHB09], Madlener et al. introduces the RecDEVS MoC, which is an extension of the original DEVS formalism to cover reconfiguration available in modern hardware architectures. The fundamental concept of RecDEVS MoC is to represent the reconfigurable hardware blocks as atomic DEVS components. Additionally, a dedicated network executive (i.e. a special kind of atomic component) is introduced, which is responsible for the reconfiguration of the system.

RecDEVS eliminates the connection connection based communication exploited by DEVS, but instead, a message based communication scheme will be used. Thus, each component available in the system has its own unique identifier and may create up to m communication messages at a single point in time. Note that m is the number of currently instantiated components within the system. Thus, the network executive has to manage a special communication bus wherein up to to $m \times m$ messages may occur at one point in time. Interestingly, the reconfiguration task was moved from the functional domain into the communication domain by defining a set of reconfiguration messages. Therefore, the reconfiguration is completely encapsulated within the network executive and the participating atomic components.

However, reconfiguration is not in the scope of this thesis. Therefore, this topic will not be detailed, but the interested reader will find more information in [MHB09].

2.4 Graphical Representation

The notation of SynDEVS models in terms of a mathematical notation is good for a definition in terms of the highest possible degree of preciseness. However, the readability of the models are weak and it is quite hard to get a fast impression what the models behaviour are. Thus, a better approach of defining SynDEVS models should be introduced to increase the readability. Other popular MoCs (e.g. AToM^3 [DV02], Ptolemy II [Lee09], or UML StateCharts [Har87]) are usually exploiting the visual programming paradigm of accomplish this task, cf. [ABZ92] for an excellent overview of programming paradigms. Therefore, an alternative approach of defining SynDEVS models is presented in terms of the visual programming paradigm. Its main goal is to simplify the definition and readability of SynDEVS models while keeping the preciseness of the graphical notation compared to the mathematical notation at its utmost. Another goal is to eliminate the need of entering repetitive information within the models (e.g. entering assignments of unused variables to ◇) by defining some simple yet powerful default rules for the models behaviour. Furthermore, the graphical user interface presented later on in Chapter 5 exploits this visual programming approach of SynDEVS models to exemplify its effectiveness.

2.4.1 Parallel Components

The graphical notation of SynDEVS parallel components focus on the readability of the communication structure in between the sub components (i.e. the port couplings defined by C_{in}, C_{out}, and C_{inner}). Thus, the notation represents the parallel component itself as a box where the sub components are placed inside. Input ports of parallel components are represented by the symbol $\triangleright$ with an annotation of port name nearby and the arrowhead is pointing inside the component. Output ports are almost the same like input ports but their arrowhead is pointing outside the component. Thus, the arrow visualize the port type (i.e. input or output). The port couplings are drawn as lines, sometimes with an arrowhead to further visualize the data flow from the source port to the sink. Examples for the intuitive use of the graphical notation are given in Figure 2.1 and Figure 2.9 which are self-explanatory and not discussed further for brevity.

2.4.2 Atomic Components

The graphical notation of SynDEVS atomic components is more complex than the notation of parallel components. However, they are defined with the goal in mind to be, both, intuitive and powerful as comparable state machine based notations (e.g. UML StateCharts [Har87]).

SynDEVS atomic components are represented as digraphs with three different kind of edges, one for each type of transition, and some further developed node notation to handle SynDEVS specific features like state timeout values. The states of an atomic SynDEVS component are represented by nodes. A node must contain the state name and its associated timeout value. Additionally, if variable assignments exists, they have to be annotated to the node[3]. Figure 2.12 depicts the graphical notation of states with and without variable assignments. The assignment box may be omitted if a state has no variable assignments (i.e. $v_i = \diamond$ for all variables $v_i \in V$). Furthermore, if variable assignments are annotated the assignments with the $\diamond$ (i.e. $v_i = \diamond$) may be left out.

---

[3] Sometimes these assignment boxes are skipped in the presented examples, if they are not needed for the understanding of the example.

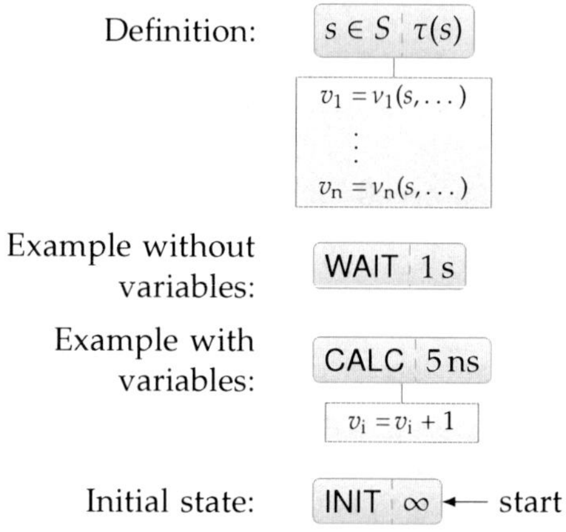

Figure 2.12 Graphical notation of states. The variable assignments are annotated at the nodes. If no variable assignments are at hand then the assignment box is omitted.

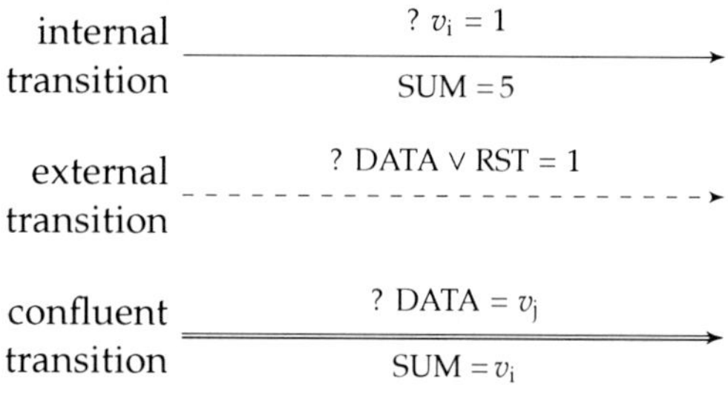

Definition:

$$s \in S \mid \tau(s)$$
$$v_1 = v_1(s, \dots)$$
$$\vdots$$
$$v_n = v_n(s, \dots)$$

Example without variables:

$$\boxed{\text{WAIT} \mid 1\,\text{s}}$$

Example with variables:

$$\boxed{\text{CALC} \mid 5\,\text{ns}}$$
$$v_i = v_i + 1$$

Initial state:

$$\boxed{\text{INIT} \mid \infty} \longleftarrow \text{start}$$

Figure 2.13 Edge types of the graphical notation for the different SynDEVS transition types

internal transition

$$\frac{?\, v_i = 1}{\text{SUM} = 5} \longrightarrow$$

external transition

$$\frac{?\, \text{DATA} \vee \text{RST} = 1}{} \dashrightarrow$$

confluent transition

$$\frac{?\, \text{DATA} = v_j}{\text{SUM} = v_i} \Longrightarrow$$

The different edges to be used for the transitions are depicted in Figure 2.13. Internal transitions are drawn like normal directed edges, external transitions are drawn dashed, and confluent ones with a double line. Output events are annotated at the edges as an assignment to the output port with "=" (e.g. SUM = 5). Both, values or variables may be used within the assignment. Thus, SUM = 5 outputs an event with value 5 over the $P_{\text{out,SUM}}$ output port and SUM = v_i transmits an event with the current value of variable v_i.

Additionally, conditions which guard the transition may be annotated. Conditionals are prefixed by the "?" symbol and, then, the transitions are only executed if the annotated condition holds true. A condition at an internal transition may contain only references to variables. However, a condition annotated at the other transition types may contain references to variables and input ports. If a condition should only check that an input port received an event regardless of the event value only the input port name is annotated (e.g. DATA). Nevertheless, a condition can check if an input port received an event with a specific event value (e.g. RST = 1) or if the event value is the same like a variable (e.g. DATA = v_j). Due to the annotation of conditions at the transitions, it is possible to define two transitions whose conditions hold true for the same system state (i.e. current state, variable data, and received events). Thus, model checking must be employed to not create models with such an indeterminism. It may be possible to transform such an indeterministic model into a deterministic one likewise the transformation of indeterministic into deterministic finite state machines. However, as the mathematical notation of SynDEVS and original DEVS only allows the entry of deterministic models this is not further evaluated.

The graphical representation of the transition functions δ_{int}, δ_{ext}, and δ_{con} need not to be completely drawn. If the graphical representation would include an edge for every single transition it would look confusing as at least three different edges would leave each node. Thus, the following simplification rules are defined to ease the modelling:

1. If the destination state of the transition is the same like the source (i.e. a loop) then the transition may be omitted within the graphical notation. By doing so, the model stays in its current state when a situation arise which is not considered.

2. If only a single internal or external transition is leaving a state then implicitly, a confluent transition with the same condition, source state, and destination state is included.

Obviously, the first rule removes unneeded information from the graphical representation. However, the second rule is a contradiction of the first rule but make sense in terms of error-prone modelling. Usually, an internal or external transition must be modelled together with an equal confluent transition to reach the desired behaviour. Consider the case that a model contain some state to calculate temporary data which is left over an internal transition. An external event would make the model to re-enter the calculation state without the implicit confluent transition. However, the second rule does not disallow this type of behaviour if desired. If the confluent transition should re-enter the state it has to be modelled explicitly as a loop. Then, the second rule will not be applied as more than two transitions are leaving the state.

The second rule was introduced while gaining practical experience with SynDEVS modelling. More than one model failed during development due to missing confluent transitions. Mostly, timeout states were not left due to periodic received events which were not considered before. Sometimes, wait states were not left over an external transition as the timeout was wrongly defined (i.e. $\tau(s) \neq \infty$). Thus, to ease error-free modelling, this rule was introduced in the design flow discussed in the later sections.

CHAPTER 3
Modelling and Validation

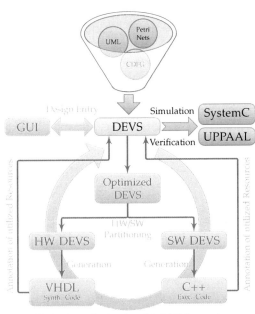

Designing cyber-physical or embedded systems is a complex task with a lot of difficulties. Usually, they are constructed as a network of heterogeneous components with strict real-time requirements. The components are working either stand-alone (i.e. an embedded system) or in collaboration with other systems while interacting with the physical world (i.e. a cyber-physical system). Even more, the system level design complexity is increasing and traditional design flows like a software/hardware co-design flow solely using C and VHDL are not capable to keep up with this demanding technology in terms of modelling the system with a high design complexity. This gap is called the *system level design gap*. In [EMD09], a possible solution is presented which could close this gap by increasing the abstraction of system level design. The fundamental concept is that a highly abstract system level design enriches the design flow in such a way, that more complex designs are feasible to create within a shorter design time compared to traditional design flows. Such an increase of abstraction was successfully performed multiple times in the software domain (e.g. transition from assembler to a high-level programming language or from a pure sequential programming languages to a pseudo-concurrent execution with threads). However, these approaches may be suitable for software but are not feasible for an embedded system or cyber-physical system, cf. [Lee08]. Thus, Lee there proposes a design flow using MoC as the foundation:

> For the next generation of cyber-physical systems, it is arguable that we must build concurrent models of computation that are far more deterministic, predictable, and understandable. Threads take the opposite approach. They make programs absurdly non-deterministic, and rely on programming style to constrain that non-determinism to achieve deterministic aims.

Jantsch defined three different approaches to handle design complexity within system level design [Jan04, pp. 21]. These are domains, hierarchy, and abstraction and will be discussed in more detail.

Hierarchy: The model is hierarchically split into different parts such that each part at a lower abstraction level reveals more detail.

Abstraction: Each abstraction level define and use different modelling concepts and semantics. Thus, a higher abstraction levels hides (irrelevant) information of the model, while a less abstract model at the lowest level is manufacturable.

Domains: The model is split into different domains. Each domain can be analysed by its own. Thus, each domain focus on a single design aspect (e.g. deadlock-free communication).

SynDEVS natively implements a hierarchical modelling approach by exploiting parallel and atomic components. Thus, a model may be designed in such a way that each sub-component of the model reveals more detailed information.

However, the other both approaches, abstraction and domains, are harder to achieve. Usually, a lot of decision making is involved in between different abstraction levels. This may include tedious hand-crafted design processes like creating a hardware / software communication interface during a refinement step of a hardware / software co-design flow. Thus, SynDEVS allows the use of automatic transformations and refinement steps to anticipate most of these hand-crafted design process steps. Even more, many different MoC may be automatically transformed into SynDEVS. Therefore, a domain-based modelling approach may be used as a starting point for modelling the system.

3.1 Model Creation

SynDEVS models may be created from scratch by using the GUI which will be introduced in Chapter 5 or by using (semi-) automatic model transformations to allow for a domain-based modelling of the system behaviour. In this section, the different methods to create SynDEVS models are highlighted.

3.1.1 Model Transformations

The different abstraction layers utilized in embedded systems design flows are illustrated in Figure 3.1. Low level implementation languages like VHDL or embedded systems C++ build the bottom layer of the abstraction pyramid. This layer features fine-granular models but a low degree of abstraction. In many ways, this abstraction level is too low to provide a satisfying design flow. Thus, SystemC with TLM[1] was introduced to raise the abstraction level with the goal to provide a combined design flow for hardware and software. Nowadays, SystemC has become a de facto standard for system level design and together with TLM, it gains

---

[1] *Transaction-Level Modelling*

Figure 3.1 Abstraction pyramid illustrating the different layers utilized in embedded systems design flows. Lower layers detail fine-granular models in terms of implementation but for the cost of abstraction. [MMH09b]

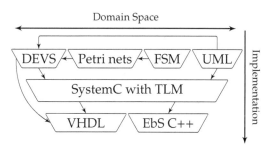

more and more momentum. Such a high-level design language build the middle layer of the abstraction pyramid. While being good at combined hardware and software development, it is still a programming language without an inherent MoC. However, a lot of scientific work has been done and different commercial tools are available on the market to improve integrated design flows from high-level languages such as SystemC down to both, embeddable software programs and synthesizable hardware.

Additionally, introduction of abstract MoCs into the design flow are even more beneficial [MMH09b]. First, a representation of a system model by exploiting diverse abstract MoCs is not limited by the features of a specific programming language like SystemC. Second, consideration of existing MoCs within the design flow preserve and allows to reuse once gained knowledge, which was aggregated for this specific model. Thirdly, the partitioning of the design problem into different problem areas, which may be tackled with different MoCs, will considerably ease the system development. These MoCs represent the top layer of the abstraction pyramid. By doing so, the system design is represented by an aggregation of various MoC, each best suited for a specific design task or aspect. Then, these models are mapped to other MoC or programming languages for executable or synthesizable code generation.

In [MMP10], a model transformation is defined as follows:

> A model transformation is the conversion of one model (source) into another model (target) using a set of rules. The rules map concepts and relations from the source meta model to the target meta model's concepts and relations. A special case of model transformation is the code generation, that enable a model to be executable. This transformation is called *model-to-text*, and is based in a set of templates rather than in a set of rules.

Both aspects, model-to-model and model-to-text transformation, are further detailed in [MMH09b]. Model transformations may be distinguished by being either a vertical (i.e. model-to-text) or a horizontal (i.e. model-to-model) transformation, cf. Figure 3.1 for some possible model transformation paths. A vertical or model-to-text transformation generates code which is executable or synthesizable. Thus, it is a specialization from an abstract model into a more fine-grained implementation comprising the target platform architecture. Usually, different aspects of the source MoC are transformed in terms of using a set of templates instead of generic transformation rules. For instance, within a vertical transformation from SynDEVS to VHDL, an event with an unsigned integer value may be represented by an unsigned signal representing the event's value and additionally, a std_logic signal to denote that an event occurred. Even more, vertical transformation templates involve the targeted architecture and, thus, must be adapted for each exploited architecture. Creating vertical transformations is a tedious process and error-prone task due to its template nature. Thus, it may not be desirable to create vertical transformations for each exploited MoC within the design flow. It is better to transform all of them horizontally into a single MoC and from there, transform them vertically down to a more detailed executable or synthesizable model.

Horizontal or model-to-model transformations allows the representation of the model's behaviour of the source MoC by another model of the targeted MoC with equivalent behaviour. A very good target MoC for these horizontal transformation is the DEVS MoC. It is highly flexible and can be easily transformed into executable and synthesizable code in terms of SynDEVS MoC with an equivalent behaviour. Even more, several MoCs can be easily expressed by DEVS. This fact has already been exploited by different scientific works: An UML state chart transformation to DEVS is presented in [RMZ+07] and a Petri net conversion is described by [BKV04], just to name a few.

Please note that it may not be sufficient to have only a single vertical transformation within the design flow. Depending upon the used MoCs, they may build different disjoint classes, where each instance of a class can only be transformed into other MoCs from the same class. For instance, a MoC with a continuous time foundation cannot be directly transformed into another MoC exploiting a discrete time base. Thus, for each MoC class, a vertical transformation for at least one representative MoC must be defined. Then, models from the diverse utilized MoCs may be horizontally transformed into models of the representative MoC and, afterwards, refined into executable and synthesizable models by solely using the rep-

Figure 3.2 Abstraction pyramid illustrating the exploited transformation paths of the AutoVision example [MMH09b]

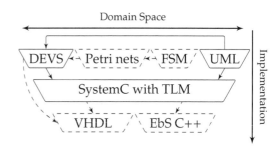

resentative's vertical transformations.

In [MMH09b], a detailed analysis of this MoC-based design flow is presented. Therefore, a complex example from the automotive domain was implemented and evaluated by Madlener et al. The AutoVision example [CSH07] consists of different components for vision enhancement and automated object recognition in the field of driving assistance. For a detailed description of the different components, which are exploited within the model, see [MMH09a, MMH09b]. However, the AutoVision example was utilized to analyse the simulation performance of the resulting executable models after model transformations. Figure 3.2 illustrates the different transformation paths which were exploited. As a starting point, an UML model of the AutoVision example was constructed using the commercial Rhapsody UML modelling tool. Afterwards, two executable SystemC SynDEVS models were created by transformation of the original UML model. First, the UML model was horizontally transformed into a DEVS model and, consecutively, vertically transformed into an executable SystemC simulation model. The horizontal transformation utilise model-to-model transformation rules while in contrast, the vertical transformation exploit the SynDEVS SystemC extension (i.e. model-to-text templates) presented later on in Section 3.3. Second, the UML model was directly transformed vertically into an executable SystemC simulation model by hand. Then, the UML model and both SystemC models were simulated. Figure 3.3 depicts the different simulation times in addition to the simulated number of model events. The UML model execution within the commercial Rhapsody UML modelling tool is about two times faster compared to the SystemC simulation models. This is highly reasonable because of the higher simulation abstraction of the plain UML simulation, which does not support the same level of concurrency compared to SystemC and SynDEVS models. Thus, a simulation with a higher abstraction is less complex

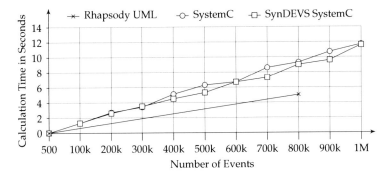

Figure 3.3 Simulation results for different executable models of the AutoVision example [MMH09b]

and therefore faster. However, by looking at the simulation times of both SystemC-based simulation models, it can be clearly seen, that the introduction of additional horizontal transformations can be performed without any substantial overhead. Thus, a design flow based solely on MoC mappings is feasible and may be exploited in terms of automatic model transformations without any negative impact on the resulting model.

3.1.2 State-Based Models of Computation

State-based MoC (e.g. Petri nets, UML state charts, or finite state machines) may be transformed into equivalent SynDEVS models in terms of their input / output behaviour due to the state-based description of atomic components. Usually, transformation rules may be easily defined for simple MoC (e.g. Moore machines) but complexity increase for more sophisticated MoC (e.g. UML state charts).

Figure 3.4 depicts two example models of commonly used finite state machine types. Firstly, a Moore machine model is defined in a) and, secondly, the Moore machine is transformed into an equivalent Mealy machine which is shown in b). These state-based models, which are defined by an untimed MoC, may be easily transformed into equivalent SynDEVS models. Thus, only an informal description of the transformation process is given instead of a formal transformation algorithm.

Figure 3.5 shows the transformation result of both models. The transformation result in the same model but with different initial states, depicted by the *Moore start* and *Mealy start* annotation. For every state s_i of the source

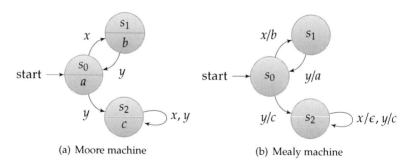

(a) Moore machine   (b) Mealy machine

Figure 3.4 Example models of common finite state machine types

Figure 3.5 Resulting Syn-
DEVS model after trans-
formation of Moore and
Mealy machines given
in Figure 3.4

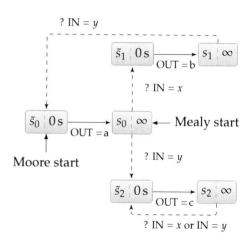

model, two states $\tilde{s}_i$ and s_i have to be created in the target model. The first
state $\tilde{s}_i$ will handle the output and the second state s_i will wait for the next
input. The output state $\tilde{s}_i$ is directly connected to the corresponding wait
state s_i in terms of an internal transition. However, for every transition
from s_i to s_j of the source model, an external transition at the target model
from s_i to $\tilde{s}_j$ must be introduced. The source model's transition conditions
may be reused unchanged. Thus, Moore and Mealy models and likewise
many other state-based models may be easily transformed into SynDEVS
models without state or transition explosion (i.e. target state count is only
increasing linearly).

More complex state-based models may be transformed to SynDEVS as

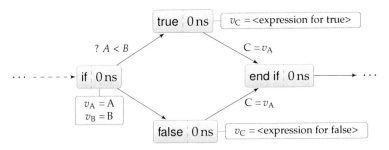

Figure 3.6 Implementation example of control flow within SynDEVS

well. In [RMZ$^+$07], a transformation from UML state charts to DEVS
state machines is described. Additionally, a transformation from UML
2.0 class diagrams and state charts to DEVS atomic components is depicted
in [SV11]. Moreover, in [RDM$^+$09], executable UML by exploiting DEVS is
described and the integration of simulation capabilities in SysML[2] by using
DEVS is outlined by [NDA10].

3.1.3 Control and Data Flow

Control and data flow may be expressed inartifically in SynDEVS models without any special transformation rule effort. Control flow may be
implemented in terms of transition conditions likewise in common au-
tomaton notations. However, implementing control flow in these notations usually requires an occurrence of events to switch states (i.e. clock
or input events). In contrast, SynDEVS states may be modelled with zero-
timeout (i.e. $\tau(s) = 0$ ns) and, thus, switching through a control path containing only zero-timeout states may be implemented without requiring additional clock or input events. Data flow may be expressed on two different
abstraction levels. First, data flow on a high abstraction level (e.g. data de-
pendencies of a complex cryptographic operation like elliptic curve scalar
point multiplication) may be established by creating parallel components
with connection in between the components. One parallel component may
represent the scalar point multiplication but exploit inner parallel components to achieve the complex operation by repeated point doubling and
addition, which themselves may exploit a finite field arithmetic atomic
component. Second, data flow on a lower abstraction level with more

---

[2] *Systems Modelling Language*

implementation details (e.g. a finite field arithmetic operation) may be expressed in terms of the state variable computations of an atomic component. Thus, within an atomic component, both, data and control flow may be expressed.

Figure 3.6 depicts a part of a SynDEVS atomic component implementing control and data flow in terms of a zero-timeout state chain. Depending on the values received over the input ports A and B, a different output may be emitted at the output port C. The value to be emitted is temporarily stored at the variable v_C and, thus, must not be calculated within a single state. Both, the calculation of v_C within the states true and false could be spanned over multiple states possibly including additional control paths. As a result, those control or data flow paths exploiting zero-timeout state chains could be seen as a single complex meta state. Thus, zero-timeout states are an important intrinsic property of SynDEVS models to express control and data flow.

3.2 Validation of DEVS Models

There is a great amount of simulation software for DEVS MoC available, [DEV11] features a comprehensive overview. These simulators feature different implementation technologies, e.g., *PyDEVS* [BV01] (Python), *DEVSJAVA* [SS04] (Java), SmallDEVS [JK06] (Smalltalk), or *ADEVS* [Nut99] (C++), but neither simulator can be easily interfaced to a common high-level modelling and simulation language like SystemC or VHDL, which is inevitable for system level design. However, the *DEVS Standardization Group* [DEV11] is a joint effort of different researchers to deal with these interoperability issues. Much work has been published regarding the integration of the different DEVS modelling and simulation tools, e.g., [ZHS99] describes how to exploit DEVS within HLA[3] [Sim00] compliant simulation frameworks. Recently, the interoperability issues of DEVS simulators were tackled, e.g. DEVS/OSGi [PUS11] and DEVS/SOA [WWZ+11] propose methods to run DEVS simulations within a heterogeneous distributed simulation environment. However, no work has been published from the research group regarding DEVS simulation in terms of system level design languages like SystemC or VHDL.

---

[3] *High Level Architecture*

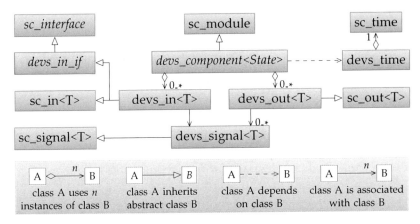

Figure 3.7 UML class diagram for the SynDEVS SystemC extension

3.3 DEVS MoC Simulation with SystemC

Integration of DEVS MoC within a system level design language such as
SystemC is very beneficial. On the one hand, it allows the simulation of
DEVS models in the context of EDA[4]. Thus, DEVS models can be simulated
with existing hardware and software description of system components
on different abstraction layers, e.g. highly abstract simulation by further
exploiting TLM or very close to the targeted implementation architecture
in terms of RTL[5] simulation.

A SystemC-based simulation of DEVS MoC combines an advanced high-
level simulation environment with MoC specific properties. Therefore, the
SynDEVS methodology was integrated into the stock OSCI[6] SystemC 2.2
kernel [Sys06] in terms of a non-intrusive kernel extension [MMH09a].
Thus, the proposed extension can exploit every SystemC implementation
which is compliant to the OSCI SystemC 2.2 standard. Figure 3.7 depicts the
classes in UML notation of the introduced non-intrusive SystemC extension
for SynDEVS simulation. In the following, this systematic approach of
integrating a MoC into SystemC will be further detailed.

Three important properties of the DEVS MoC have to be integrated
in SystemC, which are time representation, event-based communication

---

[4] *Electronic Design Automation*

[5] *Register Transfer Level*

[6] *Open SystemC Initiative*

implementation, and behavioural execution. These properties cannot be mapped directly to SystemC and, thus, solutions were developed to emulate their behaviour with the stock SystemC 2.2 kernel.

3.3.1 Time Representation

The time notation is strictly discrete and finite within SystemC. However, SynDEVS require the notation of infinite time and, thus, SystemC must be extended to include such an infinite time notation. A straight-forward approach would be to implement that special time symbol by semantically equalise it to one of the 64 bit SystemC time values (e.g. $\infty \overset{!}{=} 2^{64} - 1$). By doing so, such an approach would result in an erroneous execution of the SynDEVS Model due to wrong time arithmetic implemented by the **sc_time** class (e.g. $\infty + 1 = 0 \neq \infty$). Therefore, a class **devs_time** was introduced to handle the normal discrete, finite time but includes an additional symbol for notation of infinite time. Special care must be taken to not loose this additional timing information in terms of the normal C++ down-casting. Thus, if one would implement the new **devs_time** class by inheriting **sc_time** then a **devs_time** object set to infinite time could be automatically down-casted to **sc_time** object. This undesired down-cast would result in an object *not* representing infinite time. Therefore, the **devs_time** class is implementing **sc_time** as a member variable and includes an additional flag describing if this object is representing infinite time. Additionally, the standard arithmetic operators +, -, *, and / were overloaded to handle mixed **devs_time** and **sc_time** arithmetic correctly (e.g. $5 + \infty = \infty$).

3.3.2 Event-based Communication Implementation

For the DEVS-based event driven communication one may exploit SystemC ports (e.g. **sc_in**<T> or **sc_out**<T>) and signals (i.e., **sc_signal**<T>) but only with a slight modification of the default SystemC event handling behaviour. Specifically, the stock behaviour of a **sc_signal**<T> is to not retransmit events to a SystemC input port if an output port has written the same value twice on the signal. Thus, the default event behaviour of SynDEVS (i.e., transmission of the same event value each spawns an input event at the receiver port) could not be mapped directly to SystemC ports and signals. A simple solution would be to extend the event value with some kind of unique value (e.g. the current SystemC delta cycle) to force

SystemC to retransmit the event. However, this would result in a significant overhead of communication data within the SystemC simulator which would lead to longer simulation runtimes and higher memory footprints. Thus, a more sophisticated approach was implemented.

The main idea is to provide a SynDEVS specific subclass inherited from **sc_signal**<T> which emits events to all registered input ports whenever a value is written to the port, regardless of the event value, cf. Listing 3.1.

Listing 3.1 **devs_signal**<T> class for proper behaviour of SynDEVS events

```
1 template<class T> class devs_signal : public sc_signal<T> {
2 public:
3   devs_signal() : last_write_delta(~sc_dt::UINT64_ONE) {
4   }
5
6   virtual const sc_event& default_event() const {
7     return devs_event;
8   }
9
10  void write( const T& val) {
11    sc_signal<T>::write(val);
12    if (last_write_delta != sc_delta_count())
13      pre_last_write_delta = last_write_delta;
14    last_write_delta = sc_delta_count();
15    devs_event.notify(SC_ZERO_TIME);
16  }
17
18  virtual bool event() const {
19    if (sc_delta_count() == last_write_delta) {
20      // special case: read after write occured before.
21      return (sc_delta_count() == pre_last_write_delta + 1);
22    }
23    return (sc_delta_count() == last_write_delta + 1);
24  }
25
26 protected:
27   sc_event devs_event;
28 private:
29   sc_dt::uint64 last_write_delta , pre_last_write_delta;
30 };
```

Attention must be paid to the special case when one SystemC process is writing a new value to a signal before another SystemC process is trying to read that new value from the signal (i.e. checking if an event occurred on the signal), cf. Line 19 ff. of Listing 3.1. Within SystemC the execution order of all parallel processes is non-deterministic. Thus, an output port could emit an event (i.e. writing the event value to the signal) after another input port checks if an event occurred. In that case, the reading process would not get notified about the event because the signal would only notify input ports about the occurrence of the new event in the following delta cycle. However, by introducing that special case within the event() function the process properly informs the input ports about the event and, thus, implementing the proper behaviour of SynDEVS events.

3.3.3 Behaviour Execution

Atomic SynDEVS components are represented by the abstract class **devs_-component**<State>. The main purpose of this class is the execution of the SynDEVS model's behaviour. In contrast, the structure of the SynDEVS model can be represented by the stock SystemC class sc_module implementing the SynDEVS specific input and output ports (i.e. **devs_in**<T> and **devs_out**<T> used together with **devs_signal**<T>). However, the atomic components must inherit the **devs_component**<State> class which relevant parts are depicted below in Listing 3.2.

Listing 3.2 Partial class definition of **devs_component**<State> for implementing SynDEVS atomic components

```
1 template<class State> class DEVS_Component : public sc_module {
2 public:
3    SC_CTOR(DEVS_Component);
4    // Model-generic functions
5 private:
6    void devs_confluence_transition(void);
7    void devs_external_transition(void);
8    void devs_internal_transition(void);
9    void devs_advance(void);
10   void devs_timeout(void);
11   // Model-specific functions
12 protected:
13   virtual State initialize(void) const=0;
14   virtual void register_input_ports(void) const=0;
15   virtual void output(const State&) const=0;
16   virtual devs_time time_advance(const State&) const=0;
17   virtual State external_transition(const State&, const devs_time&)
         const=0;
18   virtual State internal_transition(const State&) const=0;
19   virtual State confluence(const State&, const devs_time&) const=0;
20   Rest of the class definition is omitted for brevity...
21 };
```

During transformation from a SynDEVS model to a SystemC simulation model, the SynDEVS model's behaviour has to be put into a derived class in terms of supplying the output and state transition functions which are defined as pure-virtual, abstract functions at the base class. Thus, the SystemC implementation of the SynDEVS model highly reflects the mathematical notation of atomic components in a clearly readable way, compare the graphical notation of the model depicted in Figure 3.9 to the SystemC notation given in Appendix A.2.

All elements of the formal SynDEVS definition are directly mapped into class functions but the model's state space is set by a template parameter. Thus, the state transition (δ_{int}, δ_{ext}, and δ_{con}), output (λ), and time advance (τ) functions can be defined by using the template parameter instead of a model-specific state space. Otherwise, it would circumvent the approach of providing a generic, abstract base class for atomic components. Moreover, all these functions are defined as **const** classes and, thus, they may not change member variables of the class directly. These functions may be executed in parallel, as discussed later in this section, which make them vulnerable to side-effects and deadlocks. Thus, it is of utmost importance to provide deadlock and side-effect free model implementations. Therefore, these functions are declared **const** to provide a model framework which enforces the developer to encode these functions side-effect and deadlock free (e.g. it is not possible to use a shared object variable within multiple transition functions).

However, it cannot be ensured that these models (i.e. transition functions) are completely dead-lock and side-effect free as the programming language C++ allows different ways of circumvention (e.g. declaring shared object variables **mutable** which may be even written inside **const** functions). Unfortunately, this is an intrinsic property of the language C++ and often exploited by the stock SystemC 2.2 implementation.

3.3.4 Model Elaboration and Simulation

SynDEVS models implemented by using the described classes have a similar elaboration and simulation cycles compared to normal SystemC modules.

In the first phase, elaboration of the parallel and atomic components took place. Parallel components are implemented as stock `sc_module` exploiting the **devs_in**<T>, **devs_out**<T>, and **devs_signal**<T> classes. Therefore, as these classes inherit stock SystemC classes, the normal Sys-

Figure 3.8 Simulation cycle of SynDEVS atomic components within SystemC

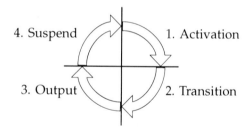

temC elaboration phase is utilized. However, for atomic components the special function `register_input_ports()` is called to register all input ports of the atomic components. Internally, the **`devs_component`**<State> class has to be informed about each input port to be able to react on received events by calling the components external or confluent functions.

In the second phase, the simulation is executed. The simulation cycle is depicted in Figure 3.8. It can be divided into four basic steps:

1. determine all components to be activated either by receiving an external event or by timeout of their current state;

2. calculate the components follow-up states by executing the required transition functions;

3. iff an internal transition function was executed, emit output events by calling the `output(state)` function;

4. register the new timeout values of the components' newly states and suspend execution until that point in time is reached.

The SystemC methodology requires that all changing port outputs are stable within a single simulation delta cycle (i.e. an evaluation of signal values followed by an update [BDB+10]). Thus, the simulation cycle of SynDEVS atomic components are embedded into a single SystemC delta cycle. Therefore, the simulated system's global state is retained stable at any point in time: All atomic components compute their output simultaneously in respect to their received input events and current component state. Then, the computed values are transmitted in terms of events to the sinks in the next SynDEVS simulation cycle (i.e. within the next single SystemC delta cycle).

The SynDEVS SystemC simulation extension utilizes three different execution models for transition functions to further test the correct implementation of the model's behaviour. These execution models modify the order and calculation of the transition functions within step 2 of the SynDEVS simulation cycle:

Needed Serial: Only one of the three transition functions is executed. During step 1 of the SynDEVS simulation cycle, it is evaluated which transition has to be evaluated for setting the next state of the atomic component. Thus, it is analysed which event types (i.e. internal, external, and confluent) occurred, cf. Listing 3.3[7].

Listing 3.3 Determination of event occurrences leading to component activation

```
216   void devs_advance(void) {
217     State nextState;
218     bool extTransitionOccured = false;   // will be true if a
                external transition occured
219     bool intTransitionOccured = false;   // will be true if a
                internal transition occured
220     std::list<devs_in_if*>::iterator it;
221     intTransitionOccured = (time_advance(curState) ==
                devs_elapsed_time());
222     // scan over all input ports and look if one got an event.
223     for (it = listInputs.begin(); (it != listInputs.end()) && !
                extTransitionOccured; it++) {
224       if ((*it)->event())
225         extTransitionOccured = true;
226     }
```

First, it will be evaluated if the elapsed time since last activation equals $\tau(s)$ of the current state s. If this holds true an internal event occurred and an internal or confluent transition has to be executed. Second, all input ports will be analysed if an event was received by one of the external ports. Afterwards, one of the transition functions is executed, cf. Listing 3.4.

Listing 3.4 Execution of transition functions but the single one needed to determine the next state of the component

```
227   if (optimizeLevel&OPT_NEEDED_SERIAL) {
228     // serial calls to the next state functions
229     if (extTransitionOccured && intTransitionOccured) {
230       devs_confluence_transition();
231     } else if (extTransitionOccured && !intTransitionOccured) {
232       devs_external_transition();
233     } else if (intTransitionOccured && !extTransitionOccured) {
```

[7] The complete source code is included in Appendix A.1.

```
234          devs_internal_transition();
235        }
236      } else if (optimizeLevel&OPT_ALL_PARALLEL) {
```

Parallel: All three transition functions are executed in parallel. However, the normal SystemC concurrent execution methods (e.g. `sc_method`) cannot be exploited, because the evaluation of the transition function must be completed within a single delta-cycle. In contrast, an implementation reusing the SystemC methodology for parallelization of the transition function would require at least two delta-cycles: one for evaluation of all possible follow up states and one for setting the follow up state to the correct one. Thus, the parallelization is implemented by using the operating systems native *Pthreads* implementation [IEE08]. First, some helper functions are introduced to wait at the `devs_advance()` function for completion of the single transition function evaluation, cf. Listing 3.5

Listing 3.5 Definition of Pthreads helper functions

```
32 // pthread mutex and condition helpers
33 #define PRE_WAIT_FOR_COND(mutex,cond) pthread_mutex_lock(&mutex);
34 #define POST_WAIT_FOR_COND(mutex,cond) pthread_cond_wait(&cond, &
       mutex);pthread_mutex_unlock(&mutex);
35 #define POST_WAIT_FOR_COND_EXECUTED(mutex,cond,signal) while (
       parallelExecutionStatus != signal) { pthread_cond_wait(&cond,
       &mutex); } pthread_mutex_unlock(&mutex);
36 #define SIGNAL_COND_EXECUTED(mutex,cond,signal)
       pthread_mutex_lock(&mutex);parallelExecutionStatus |= signal;
       pthread_cond_broadcast(&cond);pthread_mutex_unlock(&mutex);
37 #define SIGNAL_COND(mutex,cond) pthread_mutex_lock(&mutex);
       pthread_cond_broadcast(&cond);pthread_mutex_unlock(&mutex);
```

Second, these helper functions are exploited to provide proper thread locking to wait for completion of the parallel executed transition functions, cf. Listing 3.6.

Listing 3.6 Execution of transition functions in parallel by exploiting Pthreads

```
236      } else if (optimizeLevel&OPT_ALL_PARALLEL) {
237        // clear the status variable (describes which threads
           finished their execution)
238        PRE_WAIT_FOR_COND(returnToAdvanceConditionMutex,
           returnToAdvanceCondition);
239        while (parallelExecutionStatus != ALL_EXECUTED) {
```

```
240        pthread_cond_wait(&returnToAdvanceCondition, &
                returnToAdvanceConditionMutex);
241      }
242      parallelExecutionStatus = NONE_EXECUTED;
243      // signal all threads (internal, external, confluence) to
                start their execution
244      SIGNAL_COND(advanceConditionMutex, advanceCondition);
245      // wait for the threads to be finished
246      POST_WAIT_FOR_COND_EXECUTED(returnToAdvanceConditionMutex,
                returnToAdvanceCondition, ALL_EXECUTED);
247    } else if (optimizeLevel&OPT_ALL_SERIAL) {
```

Basically, all functions are executed in parallel in non-deterministic order and afterwards, the calling function waits until completion of the worker threads. However, the transition functions (e.g. `devs_internal_transition`) cannot be called directly when using Pthreads. Thus, worker thread functions are introduced to call the transition functions, cf. Listing 3.7.

Listing 3.7 Worker thread calling the transition function when exploiting Pthreads

```
154   void devs_internal_transition_thread(void) {
155     PRE_WAIT_FOR_COND(advanceConditionMutex, advanceCondition);
156     SIGNAL_COND_EXECUTED(returnToAdvanceConditionMutex,
                returnToAdvanceCondition, INT_EXECUTED);
157     for (;;) {
158       // wait for the signal to start the execution
159       POST_WAIT_FOR_COND(advanceConditionMutex, advanceCondition)
                ;
160       // execute the internal transition function
161       if (debugLevel&DBG_INT_TRANSITION) {
162         cout << TRANSITION() << std::setw(12) << timestamp(":_")
                  << "[" << devsname() << "]_devs_internal_transition_"
                  ;
163         print(cout);
164       }
165       intState = internal_transition(curState);
166       if (debugLevel&DBG_INT_TRANSITION) {
167         cout << "_->_";
168         print(cout, intState);
169         cout << NORMAL() << endl;
170       }
171       // signal the end of executon
172       PRE_WAIT_FOR_COND(advanceConditionMutex, advanceCondition);
173       SIGNAL_COND_EXECUTED(returnToAdvanceConditionMutex,
                returnToAdvanceCondition, INT_EXECUTED);
```

174   }
175   }

At the elaboration phase, it is analysed if the component's transition function execution should be in parallel. Then, all three worker threads are started which run in an infinite loop but the execution of the transition function is only executed when signalled by the `devs_advance()` function.

A two way handshake scheme is exploited to ensure a deadlock free evaluation of transition functions. First, the worker threads have to issue that they are in a state where they can start execution of the transition functions immediately. Second, they are signalled to start the execution and the main thread waits for completion of the worker threads. Therefore, it is ensured that (I) all worker threads are ready to compute and (II) computation is finished. Thus, no deadlock can occur by using this scheme. Please note that usually a two way handshake is not sufficient for deadlock freeness. The signals to start or finish computations could be lost. However, the presented implementation exploit shared variables with mutex locking and, thus, no signal from or two the worker threads will be lost.

All Serial: All three transition functions are executed in serial but in a non-deterministic order, cf. Listing 3.8.

Listing 3.8 Serial execution of all transition functions

```
247     } else if (optimizeLevel&OPT_ALL_SERIAL) {
248       unsigned int call = 0x7, bit;
249       // Shuffle the three transition calls but execute each only
              once.
250       while (call != 0) {
251         do {
252           bit = 1 << (rand()%3);
253         } while ((call&bit)==0);
254         if (bit == 0x1) {
255           devs_internal_transition();
256         } else if (bit == 0x2) {
257           devs_external_transition();
258         } else {
259           devs_confluence_transition();
260         }
261         call &= ~bit;
262       }
263     } else {
```

Regardless of the utilized method, all variants will show the same behaviour if the SynDEVS model is defined correctly (e.g. no shared mutable
object variables). Thus, in case of a difference in behaviour, the modelling
error can be located during simulation and eliminated in terms of analysing
the simulation results and the presented debug output.

3.3.5 Performance Evaluation

The performance of the introduced SystemC extension for simulation of
SynDEVS models may be evaluated regarding two properties. First, the
simulation speed of DEVS models in comparison with other pure DEVS
simulation engines. Second, the simulation overhead in terms of a DEVS
model implemented in SystemC by exploiting the proposed extension
against a native SystemC implementation of the model by hand.

Simulation Speed

Many DEVS simulators implement the *gpt* example from [ZKP00, pp. 80].
This model allows a basic test of correct simulation functionality as this
model exploit different components running in parallel and with communication in between the model. Moreover, this model allows a comparison
of different DEVS simulators regarding their simulation performance.

Figure 3.9 depicts the exploited atomic components and their wiring,
cf. Appendix A.2 for the SystemC source code. The *Generator* component
will generate jobs with a fixed rate after receiving a start signal until it
receives a stop signal. The generated jobs will be received by the *Processor* component, processed, and retransmitted after a fixed time which is
denoted by the timeout of the PROCESS state. Both, the jobs generation
and processing rate are monitored by the *Observer* component until the
specified timeout (i.e. v_{rest}) is hit. Then, the generator is instructed to stop
process generation. Please note that the symbol ϵ is used to denote the
elapsed time of the OBSERVE state since last activation. Thus, the overall
timeout of that state is $v_{rest} = 1000\,\text{ns}$, regardless of how often the state was
re-entered in terms of receiving an external event.

Figure 3.10 depicts the simulation speed of the proposed SystemC extension in comparison to other DEVS simulators. The *gpt* model was executed
on the simulation platforms with an increasing job count and a fixed job
generation rate and job processing time. The simulation with the SystemC
extension performs best with 1.52 sec compared to PyDEVS with 5.31 sec

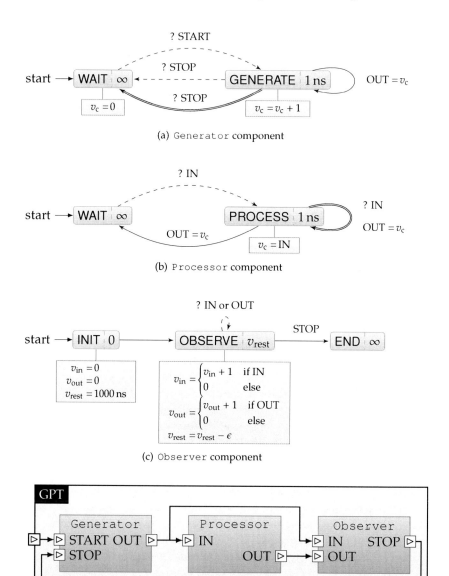

(a) `Generator` component

(b) `Processor` component

(c) `Observer` component

(d) Toplevel parallel component

Figure 3.9 Behaviour of the atomic components and structure of the toplevel parallel component exploited by the *gpt* performance evaluation example

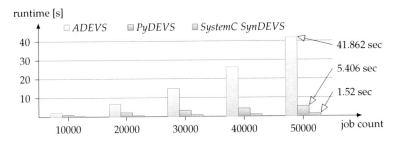

Figure 3.10 Simulation effort for the *gpt* model [MMH09a]

and ADEVS with 41.86 sec. The main reason of such a high performance boost is likely the employed optimized SystemC simulation kernel, which is more advanced than in most other simulators. Even more, from these figures can be seen that the obtained performance boost due to the exploitation of the SystemC simulation environment clearly outweighs any additional overhead introduced by the additional SystemC MoC software layer.

Simulation Overhead

In [MMH09a], the performance between a SynDEVS model exploiting the proposed SystemC extension and a native SystemC implementation is given. Therefore, the before mentioned AutoVision example was implemented and evaluated. As all components within the model are run in parallel, a fair comparison of the different execution methods may be done. Thus, the performance evaluation of this model focus on two different characteristics of the proposed SystemC extension: (I) overall simulation runtime (i.e. throughput) and (II) processing time for a single event (i.e. latency). Even more, a hand-written SystemC reimplementation of the SynDEVS model is further analysed. By doing so, the overhead introduced by exploiting the proposed SystemC extension can be quantified.

For a fair comparison of the SystemC and SynDEVS model, one has to differ between state transitions with low and high computation complexity and, thus, processing times. Then, measurements with low computation complexity will give a realistic view on how big the impact of the extension on the throughput (i.e. runtime of the model) is. Contrary, the high transition processing times will measure the impact on latency (i.e. how fast a single transition can be handled) in terms of the different execution

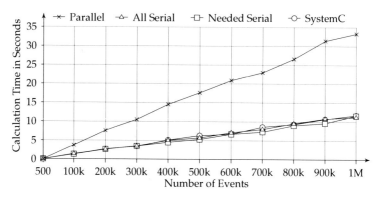

(a) Performance comparison for an increasing number of events

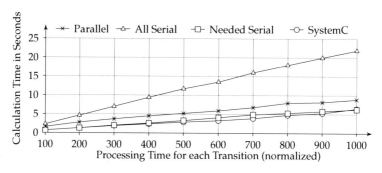

(b) Performance comparison for transitions with increasing processing time

Figure 3.11 Simulation results for the AutoVision example [MMH09a]

methods.

Figure 3.11 depict the results for a) throughput and b) latency. Simulation of the SynDEVS model by executing only a single transition function (i.e. *Needed Serial*) is comparable to the hand-written and optimized SystemC implementation. For SynDEVS models with low transition processing times, it is beneficial to use the *All Serial* method (i.e. execution of all transition functions but in serial instead of parallel). Then, the model can be simulated efficiently but modelling errors in terms of design flaws originating from synchronisation or concurrency issues can still be identified. In contrast, the *Parallel* method has a worse impact on the runtime of the model due to thread management and locking. However, when one

exploits these methods in SynDEVS models with high transition processing times, it is beneficial to prefer *Parallel* over *All Serial*. In comparison to
the high effort needed to calculate the transition functions, the overhead
for thread management and locking is negligible. Thus, SynDEVS models
can be easily implemented by exploiting the proposed SystemC extension
instead of some tedious hand-written native implementations without any
performance drawbacks.

CHAPTER 4

Hardware / Software Co-Design with SynDEVS MoC

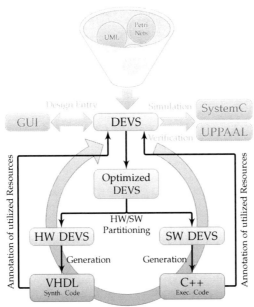

Design Space Exploration / Model Refinement

In this chapter, the hardware / software co-design flow with SynDEVS MoC is described. A large variety of work is available addressing the inherent advantages of exploiting MoCs for system level design. It raises the level of abstraction to meet the design requirements of system level design flows which is inevitable for the large growing complexity of modern embedded systems. The introduction of MoC into the system level design flow allow a more abstract view on the system. For instance, the system behaviour could be described with Petri net models and, thus, they can be used to verify whether the algorithm is deadlock free, i.e., the Petri nets liveness property can assure that the algorithm may be executed in such a way that it always terminates. Even more, an exploitation of timed MoCs may be very beneficial regarding the design of cyber physical systems because such systems have both strict time and concurrency requirements.

In [DP06], a comprehensive overview of platform-based design tools, from both, industry and academia, is given. This survey results in the fact that only a small subset of the considered tools exploit timed MoCs within their system level design flow. Usually, a timed MoC is used only in a small subset of the considered ESL[1] synthesis tools' tasks and, thus, no complete ESL design flow is covered by a single timed MoC. Recently, academic approaches for such a complete ESL design flow exploiting a single MoC are compared and discussed in [GHP+09]. The presented tools are very strong in certain synthesis aspects (e.g. design space exploration or model refinement) but do not exploit timed MoCs for the system specification. Thus, they still need to be further improved to allow for a more general use of MoCs from different domains. However, the exploited methods for a variety of synthesis aspects (e.g. design space exploration or software / hardware partitioning) may be applied to SynDEVS models as well. Please note that these aspects of the design flow are not discussed in detail within this thesis. The focus of this work is to provide a foundation for a hardware / software co-design flow based on SynDEVS models (i.e. modelling and validation of SynDEVS models with subsequent transformations to software and hardware source code). Hence, to provide a full-fledged ESL synthesis tool further methods to allow a smooth design space exploration and hardware / software partitioning, binding, and scheduling have to be incorporated.

Modelling environments, which address an exploitation of different

---

[1] *Electronic System Level*

MoCs for system level design, focus on model transformation and model interaction (e.g. Ptolemy II [BLL$^+$05]). Hence, they are usually very strong on high abstraction levels but weak on the lower levels (i.e. subsequent synthesis of the abstract model). Most of these modelling tools only cover a transformation to software source code but hardware synthesis is only limited available. In [FLN06], a limited hardware synthesis is described for some of the MoCs exploited within Ptolemy II but no hardware / software co-design has been addressed. In contrast, ForSyDe [SJ04] allows hardware / software co-design and, thus, hardware synthesis is available but only for a very small subset of the exploited MoCs (i.e. MoCs have to be based on the assumption of perfect synchronicity which restricts their approach to untimed specifications only). On the other hand, ForSyDe has been used as a foundation for the ANDRES [HOS$^+$07] design flow which is strong in both, software transformation and hardware synthesis, albeit exploited together with HetSC [HV07]. However, their methodology exploit different MoCs for hardware and software implementations. Thus, exchange of model behaviour of software and hardware instances may be done only very carefully because of the possible loss of MoC specific information during design space exploration, model refinement, and especially during hardware / software co-design.

Figure 4.1 depicts a hardware / software co-design flow based on the SynDEVS MoC (i.e. a timed MoC). Timed MoC models (i.e. SynDEVS or RecDEVS models) built the foundation of system level design flow. Entering the design flow with other MoCs is possible in terms of exploiting the model transformations methodology described in Section 3.1.1. Thus, a single SynDEVS model describes the entire design of the system under consideration. Early in the design flow, SystemC simulation, cf. Section 3.3, or UPPAAL verification [MWH10] may be used to test and verify the system behaviour. Beginning from such a single SynDEVS model, the hardware / software co-design flow may be performed. The system level design flow steps are depicted by blue boxes in Figure 4.1. These steps are divided in processes which are fully automated (i.e. right-angled boxes) and processes requiring a manual intervention of the designer (i.e. boxes with rounded-corners).

Initially, the designer has to provide a partitioning of the system model. Therefore, a set of instances may be defined and each instance has a designated implementation target which is either hardware or software. Then, each atomic component (i.e. description of the model behaviour) has to be bound to a hardware or to a software instance. Parallel components (i.e. hi-

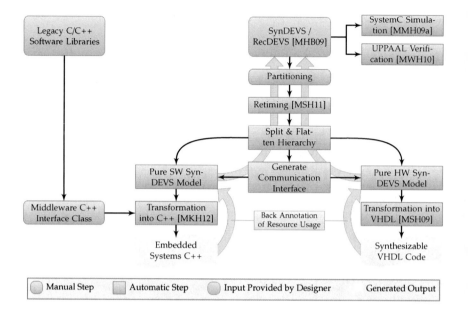

Figure 4.1 Hardware / Software Co-Design Flow for Embedded Systems based on SynDEVS MoC [MH11]

erarchical description) are not bound to instances because the model's hi-erarchy will be flattened at a later step of the design flow. Please note that an arbitrary amount of hardware and software instances may be exploited during the partitioning step.

Afterwards, the model's timing behaviour will be automatically opti-mized in terms of zero-timeout state elimination. The resulting model will only feature states with non-zero timeout annotations (i.e. $\tau(s) \neq 0$). The algorithm and the concept behind this optimization step will be described later on in Section 4.2.3.

In the next step, the single model for the entire system will be split into different models where each model will only include components of the same instance. Therefore, the hierarchy will be flattened and the connec-tions in between components of different instances will be rerouted over newly introduced toplevels' ports. This step will be detailed in Section 4.1. Even more, all connections in between software and hardware instances are rerouted over dedicated communication interfaces which will be automatically generated, cf. Section 4.3.2. After both steps are finished, the old single model is replaced by a lot of models in which each of it is representing a single target instance (i.e. each model is targeted to be implemented either as one of the software or as one of the hardware instances).

For each hardware SynDEVS model, a transformation into synthesizable VHDL will be performed. This step will be detailed later on in Section 4.2.

Similarly, for each software model, a transformation process to generate C++ source code for the model's behaviour will be exploited. This transformation process will be thoroughly described in Section 4.3. Please note that legacy C or C++ software libraries may be exploited within SynDEVS software models, too. Therefore, the designer has to provide the design flow with additional input (i.e. the source code of the libraries) and has to define a middleware C++ class for interfacing the SynDEVS model with the legacy software library.

Afterwards, the automatically generated C++ source code and VHDL source code may be compiled and synthesized for the targeted platform. Thus, common C / C++ compilers and VHDL synthesizers may be exploited (e.g. Xilinx EDK tool-suite tailored for FPGAs). Please note that the resource consumption of the models' components may be back-annotated to the original single model representing the entire system. Thus, the designer is able to consider a model refinement or partitioning change of the model at hand. Even more sophisticated design space exploration methods may be exploited which probably could automatically reconsider the initial SynDEVS model.

4.1 Hardware / Software Partitioning

Different implementation instances targeted either to be synthesized as hardware or to be compiled as software may be defined within a SynDEVS model's XML[2] file. By doing so each atomic component may be attributed with one of these instances. Thus, a partitioning of the model into distinct hardware and software instances may be defined by the designer. In subsequent steps of the design flow, all components bound to the same instance will be collected together into a single instance-dependent SynDEVS model. Connections in between hardware instances are rerouted through the toplevel ports of these newly created single SynDEVS models. In contrast, connections in between software instances or software and hardware

---

[2] *Extensible Markup Language*

Figure 4.2 A single Syn-DEVS model with two instances tailored to different hardware targets (i.e. *HW* and *HW2*)

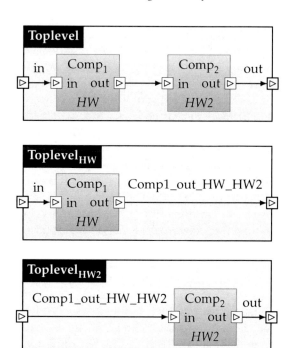

Figure 4.3 Both resulting SynDEVS models (i.e. Toplevel$_{HW}$ and Toplevel$_{HW2}$) after the automated *Split and Flatten Hierarchy* step of the design flow. Each model includes only the atomic components bound to the same target instance. Connections in between different target instances are rerouted over the toplevel parallel components' ports.

instances will exploit special communication interfaces dedicated to the exploited target architecture. For instance, FSL[3] communication interfaces are generated for the Xilinx MicroBlaze soft-core processor architecture, cf. Section 4.3.2. However, an automated communication interface generation may be exploited for connections in between hardware instances, too.

Figure 4.2 depicts a single SynDEVS model with two atomic components Comp$_1$ and Comp$_2$ which are tailored to two different hardware instances *HW* and *HW2*. This SynDEVS model has to be split into new SynDEVS models in which each model is only describing the structure and behaviour of the components bound to the same target instance, before the rest of the design flow steps may be executed. Thus, all atomic components which belong to the same target instance will be relocated into a new SynDEVS model with only a single toplevel parallel component. By doing so the component hierarchy will be flattened which is very beneficial

---

[3] *Fast-Simplex-Link*

for the software transformation process. Then, events may be passed directly from the atomic component's source port to the atomic component's destination port without consideration of complicated interconnection by parallel components. Effectively, this will decrease the computational effort of (dynamically) resolving the events destination ports during communication because the sink is always known a priori (i.e. without additional look-ups through parallel component interconnections).

Figure 4.3 depicts both automatically generated SynDEVS models for the instances *HW* and *HW2*. Unnecessary input and output ports are each removed at the toplevel parallel components and, furthermore, new ports will be introduced to represent the old interconnection of components across instance boundaries. These resulting SynDEVS models will be each processed by the rest of the necessary design flow steps until VHDL or C++ source code is automatically generated. Please note that additional communication-related components will be introduced if a SynDEVS model is split into hardware and software parts, cf. Section 4.3.2.

In the rest of this chapter, the different transformation processes for automated generation of synthesizable VHDL source code and embedded systems C++ source code will be detailed.

4.2 SynDEVS to Hardware Transformation

In order to transform a SynDEVS model to an equivalent hardware description (i.e. synthesizable VHDL source code), different transformation methodologies may be exploited [MSH09]. First, SynDEVS models may be executed in hardware in terms of exploiting an interpreter engine running in hardware, too. Thus, the complete SynDEVS model's behaviour needs to be converted into an intermediate model, with the goal in mind that this model may be easily executed by the interpretation engine solely written in synthesizable VHDL. Thus, this transformation methodology is similar to the SystemC extension discussed earlier in Section 3.3. However, such an approach may result in an inefficient hardware implementation because, both, the interpretation entity and the intermediate model, would need hardware resources. Such an approach may be more suited for a hardware / software co-design flow exploiting a domain-specific processor. Then, the interpretation engine may be implemented as a domain-specific SPU[4] while the intermediate model is executed in terms of software run-

---

[4] *Special Purpose Unit*

ning on the SPU. However, even for this mixed approach, such a SPU have to be developed for each target architecture which is a tedious and error-prone task.

Second, SynDEVS models may be completely transformed into native synthesizable VHDL source code with all SynDEVS MoC execution semantic characteristics (e.g. timing behaviour). Then, regardless of the targeted architecture, these model-to-text transformation rules would have to be defined only once. However, one has to carefully choose the exploited VHDL constructs to maximize usability among the different synthesis tools available on the market. Additionally, defining the transformation rules is complex for some aspects of SynDEVS because of the lack of a direct VHDL pendant. For instance, within SynDEVS MoC time may be directly addressed through state timeout annotations but not within synthesizable VHDL (i.e. `wait` statements are not part of the synthesizable VHDL subset).

The second approach was chosen for SynDEVS to hardware transformation. It is superior compared to the first approach in terms of resource usage, execution speed, and flexibility regarding the diversity of target platforms in heterogeneous systems. In the rest of this section, different implementation characteristics of the model-to-text transformation rules are highlighted and discussed in detail.

4.2.1 MoC to Hardware Transformation

There are many highly relevant MoC modelling environments available but most of them do not feature automatic hardware generation within their design flows. Usually, they are including some transformation into software representations only. In the latter, the most important modelling environments are discussed regarding model to hardware transformations.

The Ptolemy II [BLL+05] modelling environment supports hardware synthesis by an extension from [FLN06]. However, transformation of models from the SR domain to VHDL is only supported and, thus, it is primarily suitable for DSP[5] applications only.

HetSC [HV07] models, specified by an additional SystemC layer to ease MoC integration within SystemC, may be manually refined into synthesizable SystemC code. Thus, it does not feature an automatic model-to-text transformation process but assists the designer in doing so by hand.

ForSyDe [SJ04] allows to model a highly abstract system level design,

---

[5] *Digital Signal Processing*

which may be subsequently refined into some hardware implementation model in terms of design transformations. Afterwards, this model is mapped to the given target platform. Additionally, their presented hardware / software co-design process allows the generation of executable C code and synthesizable VHDL source code. However, ForSyDe limits the modelling fidelity of the initial system level design to computational models based on the assumption of perfect synchronicity. According to [Jan04, p. 182], for those models the following assumption has to be made:

> " Perfect synchrony hypothesis: Neither computation nor communication takes time. "

Thus, ForSyDe may not be suited for a broad application range (e.g. cyber-physical systems).

In [LKH+96], an approach of directly transforming DEVS models into VHDL source code is presented. Despite their claim of translating the complete DEVS models behaviour, only a small subset of DEVS is considered. Timing annotations within DEVS models (i.e. the state timeout function τ) are not implemented therein. Thus, by using their introduced approach, one of DEVS most intrinsic properties may not be exploited which is highly questionable.

4.2.2 SynDEVS MoC Transformation into VHDL

Most SynDEVS features may be directly represented by native VHDL constructs. However, the timing characteristic of SynDEVS models has to be carefully considered as it may not be directly transformed into synthesizable VHDL source code.

Within SynDEVS atomic components, each state s has a timeout value $\tau(s)$ annotated which may be classified into zero-timeout ($\tau(s) = 0$), real-timeout ($\tau(s) = \mathbb{R}^+ \setminus \{0, \infty\}$), and non-timeout ($\tau(s) = \infty$), cf. Table 2.1. The latter timing class (i.e. non-timeout) may be easily implemented within VHDL source code. It is almost equivalent to modelling a plain untimed FSM within VHDL source code which is well-known and doable without any obstacles. For instance, such a state machine with only untimed transition behaviour may be easily described by a single-process FSM [Rus11] within VHDL source code. Thus, state changes may be solely done in terms of receiving some external events and determine the following state upon the external event values. However, both, zero-timeout states and real-timeout states, are harder to transform. Before discussing how both timing classes are handled within the transformation process, the timing characteristics of hardware description languages like VHDL must be pointed out.

The synthesizable VHDL subset does not feature direct timing annotations within. Time is modelled by exploiting a clock signal in terms of clocked processes in which computation is described in terms of combinatorial logic between clocked registers. Thus, a synthesizable VHDL model given at this common RTL abstraction level is specified as a *clocked synchronous model*. In [Jan04, p. 199], Jantsch defines that a clocked synchronous model is based on the following assumption:

> Clocked synchronous hypothesis: There is a global clock signal controlling the start of each computation in the system. Communication takes no time, and computation takes one clock cycle.

This assumption holds true for synthesizable VHDL source code. Computation between registers may be either defined by a clocked process (i.e. explicit with registers) or by concurrent assignments (i.e. implicit without registers but connected to registers throughout the model hierarchy). Communication times (i.e. latencies of the interconnections between registers and logic elements) are not modelled. Thus, synthesizable VHDL entities are described with the assumption in mind that both, communication and computation, will take an arbitrary but yet unknown time after implementation on the target platform and which may be successfully handled on it. Regarding the timing behaviour of the VHDL model, the designer constraints the clock cycle by specifying the clock cycle's delay only. Thus, during model synthesis, the supplied model has to be synthesized into a circuit or FPGA[6] bitstream and afterwards, checked against the timing constraints. In detail, the longest path between registers inside the circuit is determined in terms of highest delay. Then, the once unknown and arbitrary delay time is now determined for the targeted platform and may be matched against the initial model constraints (i.e. the calculated circuit delay has to be smaller than the clock cycle delay specified by the designer). However, if that requirement is not met, basically, the designer has to switch to a faster target platform or refine the model to meet the timing constraint (e.g. introduce pipeline techniques inside the longest path).

Within SynDEVS, the designer may describe time at the model in terms of providing timing annotations at states. Contrary to the mentioned synthesis result delay times which describe exactly the calculation delay, a timing

---

[6] *Field Programmable Gate Array*

annotation within SynDEVS specify the latest point in time when the computation of a state has to be finished. Thus, the given timing annotation is abstract in terms that the calculation delays, achieved after implementation on the desired target platform, may be shorter (i.e. the time to complete the computation may be shorter). Therefore, timing annotations serve the purpose of defining how long a SynDEVS model should retain in a specific state and, thus, only constrain how fast the states annotated computations have to be performed.

Even more, zero-timeout states describe computations within the model where no time should pass by. In general, this concept may be compared to delta cycles used within hardware description language simulators. Within VHDL simulators, a delta cycle is exploited to calculate the final stable output value of a combinatorial logic block featuring a feedback loop. Such a stable output value may be determined under the assumption that the circuit does not feature *Zeno*-behaviour. Following the principle of delta cycles, the cycle free zero-timeout state chains may be attached to adjacent real-timeout states. Then, the delays of the calculation within zero-timeout states, introduced after implementation into hardware, may be additionally assigned to the calculation delays of the real-timeout states.

Timing Register

In [MSH09], the following approach is proposed to map the state timeouts $\tau(s)$ to synthesizable VHDL source code. The basic idea of the method is that each atomic component is transformed into a single-process FSM exploiting a timer register for handling the state timeout. After entering a real-timeout state, the register is preloaded with a timeout value of that state. At each clock cycle the timer register is decremented and the internal transition is executed iff it reaches zero. However, it is not trivial to calculate such a timer timeout value for each state because the discrete event based SynDEVS model has to be transformed into an equivalent clocked synchronous model. Therefore, the derivation of these values is detailed in the latter.

First, only SynDEVS models without zero-timeout state chains are considered. For all states of the SynDEVS model, the largest possible clock period is evaluated which is the greatest common divisor $\tau_{gcd} = \gcd(\{\tau(s)|s \in S\})$. By exploiting this common divisor, each state's timeout value may be expressed as an integer multiplied with τ_{gcd}. Then, this integer value may be directly exploited as the timer register value mentioned before.

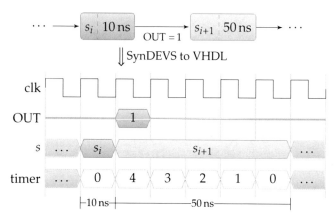

Figure 4.4 VHDL execution of a transformed SynDEVS model with real-timeout states (i.e. $\tau(s) = \mathbb{R}^+ \setminus \{0, \infty\}$)

Figure 4.4 illustrates this behaviour. For the given example, τ_{gcd} calculates to $\tau_{gcd} = gcd(10\,ns, 50\,ns) = 10\,ns$. Thus, the timer register for s_i has to be preloaded with the integer 0 and for s_{i+1} with the value 4. After synthesis, the system has to be supplied with a clock signal of $\frac{1}{10\,ns} = 100\,MHz$ and then, the single-process FSM may execute the states with the correct timeout behaviour as depicted in Figure 4.4.

Second, SynDEVS models with zero-timeout state chains are considered. Please note that these timeout chains have to be cycle free. However, this constraint is highly reasonable for SynDEVS models because otherwise, the model could feature Zeno-behaviour which is not synthesizable (i.e. infinite amount of state changes without time is passing by). As outlined at the proof of Theorem 1, the longest length n of an atomic component's zero-timeout chains may be determined. Following the idea of embedding the calculation of zero-timeout chains at adjacent non-zero-timeout states, up to n additional clock cycles for the calculation of each states variable assignments have to be reserved (i.e. at least a single clock cycle for each state of the zero-timeout chain), cf. Figure 4.5. Thus, the calculation of τ_{gcd} has to be adjusted to

$$\tau_{gcd} = \frac{gcd(\{\tau(s)|S \in S\})}{n + 1} .$$

Even for the worst case where $\tau(s)$ is minimal, up to $n + 1$ clock cycles are available for the calculation of the zero-timeout chain (i.e. n cycles with a

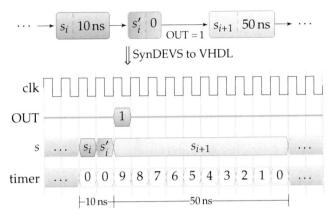

Figure 4.5 VHDL execution of a transformed SynDEVS model with real-timeout states (i.e. $\tau(s) = \mathbb{R}^+\setminus\{0, \infty\}$) and a zero-timeout state chain (i.e. $\tau(s) = 0$)

single cycle for each state of the chain) and the adjacent non-zero-timeout state (i.e. a single cycle).

However, this approach impose a high timing constraint for synthesis. The resulting synthesizable VHDL model will have a clock frequency requirement of $f_{min} = \frac{1}{\tau_{gcd}}$ which may be impossible to achieve on the target platform. Therefore, a model optimization step is introduced, significantly reducing this timing requirement, which will be detailed in Section 4.2.3, after the rest of the SynDEVS to VHDL transformation process is discussed.

Transformation Rules and Process

SynDEVS models are described by parallel and atomic components and their interconnection which have to be transformed into synthesizable VHDL source code. Parallel components solely describe the structure and, in contrast, atomic components describe the model's behaviour. All these informations of a SynDEVS model are stored together within a single XML file.

To be more specific, the SCXML[7] [LEH+08] file format type is exploited. However, some new XML tags have to be introduced to successfully store a SynDEVS model within SCXML. Thus, atomic components, ports, and

---

[7] *State Chart XML*

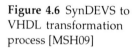

Figure 4.6 SynDEVS to VHDL transformation process [MSH09]

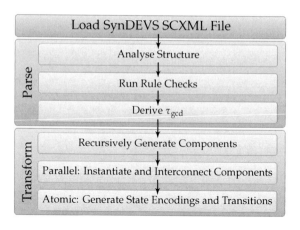

connections are stored within <**atomic**>, <**port**>, and <**connection**> tags. To handle the SynDEVS different transition types a new tag named <**transition**> was introduced with an attribute **type** to distinguish between internal, external, or confluent transitions. A more detailed description, along with some illustrative SCXML example, is featured in [MSH09].

The SynDEVS model stored as a SCXML file is the input for the transformation process as depicted by Figure 4.6. The SynDEVS model is parsed and transformed into synthesizable VHDL source code. During the parsing step, the model is analysed regarding its structure, some rule checks are performed, and afterwards, the τ_{gcd} value is calculated, cf. Section 4.2.2.

While the model's component hierarchy is parsed recursively from top to bottom, meta data for the model's components are extracted. However, all zero-timeout chains within atomic components are verified against their output port behaviour: All exploited output ports within a zero-timeout chain have to be disjunct. Thus, each output port is only written once and not multiple times within different states of the zero-timeout chain. This is of utmost importance to not violate the SynDEVS port behaviour (i.e. an output port only emits a single event at each point in time), cf. Section 2.2.1. Additionally, states are checked if outgoing internal, external, or confluent transitions are missed. In that case, implicit loop-back transitions, recall Section 2.4.2, are added to the extracted meta-data to subsequently transform a well-formed model.

Regarding the determination of the τ_{gcd} values, the designer may choose between two different approaches. The default approach is that the transformation process may calculate the required τ_{gcd} itself, cf. Section 4.2.2.

Thus, the transformation process present the timing requirement for the clock signal at the end of the process to the designer. However, this approach may be not practical when the generated VHDL source code may be used within a system level design with a fixed global clock at the target platform. Therefore, the following alternative approach may be exploited by the designer. Instead of automatically calculating the requirement for the clock signal, the designer may set the timing requirement to a fixed value as a constraint. Then, during τ_{gcd} determination, the transformation process checks if the state's timeout value can be exactly reached by using that introduced timing constraint. If it could not the reached, the designer is notified about the possible timeout clock skew. Then, either the model or the target platform with its clock constraint has to be modified.

Based on that extracted meta data, the components are transformed recursively. For each component of the model, a single VHDL entity is created.

Parallel components are transformed into basic VHDL entities which instantiate the sub-components. The connections in between the SynDEVS components are represented by VHDL signals interconnecting the instantiated entities' ports. Each port is represented by two VHDL input or output ports. One for the event value and one additional bit signal to notify if an event occurred on the port at the current point in time.

Atomic components are transformed into a VHDL entity solely containing a single-process FSM to implement the component's behaviour. For each state within the SynDEVS model, a corresponding state within the VHDL process is generated. Then, within these states, for each outgoing transition, a conditional block will be generated to switch the state and to implement the computations of the target state's assignments. Additionally, output port's assignments are generated for internal transitions only. The assignments expressions, which will be later introduced in Section 5.3, are parsed into an AST[8] and afterwards, converted into native VHDL source code by recursively walking the AST.

State timeout values are represented by the timing register introduced in the last section. The timeout values may be annotated at the SynDEVS model either by a time unit (e.g. ns, μs, ms, ...) or with the unit c to specify the discrete time steps directly. Thus, if the values are given with a time unit then the timer will be preloaded with the value derived from τ_{gcd} like mentioned before. Otherwise, the timer will be directly preloaded

---

[8] *Abstract Syntax Tree*

with the specified timeout value. It allows the designer to additionally specify state timeout values dependent on τ_{gcd}. For instance, $0\,c$ is a zero-timeout and $1\,c$ is τ_{gcd} and, thus, the smallest possible timeout achievable after implementation. This type of timeout specification is very useful if communication interfaces are to be implemented (e.g. FSL) in which some signals have to be driven for exactly one system clock cycle. By using such an artificial time unit c the designer may specify this behaviour without specific knowledge of the final system clock (i.e. to which value τ_{gcd} will be set during the transformation process). However, these timing values will be written to the timer register at the states' conditional blocks, too.

The VHDL source code generated by the transformation process is highly readable. Thus, the designer may easily cross-identify all relevant parts of the input SynDEVS model at the generated VHDL output. By doing so, the described fully automated transformation process may not be seen as a black-box process in terms of getting an unreadable output comparable to a netlist after VHDL synthesis. Therefore, this transparent transformation process is very beneficial for the designer when facing implementation issues: From the generated VHDL source code (i.e. low abstraction level point of view), the problematic SynDEVS model parts (i.e. high abstraction level point of view) may be identified easily and further optimized, fixed, or refined.

Application Example

As a proof-of-concept of the SynDEVS model to VHDL source code trans-formation process, a simple UART[9] was implemented. The UART with receiver and transmitter capabilities was created as a raw SynDEVS model and subsequently transformed into synthesizable VHDL source code. The XUPv5-LX110T Development System [Xil11b] featuring a Xilinx Virtex-5 FPGA [Xil09a] was chosen as the target platform. Thus, a MicroBlaze soft-core processor was implemented which interfaces the UART IP core over FSL. By doing so, the SynDEVS model for the UART IP core features both, a receiver and a transmitter, for serial data as well as a FSL master and slave interface. On the one hand, data received over the serial line (i.e. 115,200 baud, 8 data bits, 1 start bit, 1 stop bit and an even parity bit) is transmitted over the FSL master interface to the MicroBlaze processor. On the other hand, the processor may send data over the FSL to the IP core which is re-ceived by the FSL slave interface and, then, transmitted over the serial line.

---

[9] *Universal Asynchronous Receiver Transmitter*

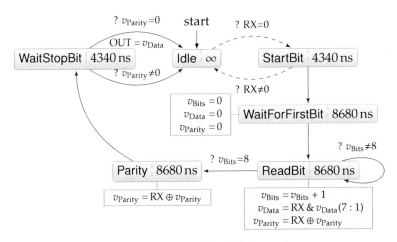

Figure 4.7 UART receiver modelled as a SynDEVS atomic component

Both, receiving and transmitting of data, may be done in parallel. Thus, the before mentioned components (i.e. FSL slave, FSL master, UART receiver, UART transmitter) were created as atomic components and interconnected in the toplevel parallel component.

The SynDEVS model was transformed into synthesizable VHDL source code and, afterwards, embedded into the Xilinx EDK design flow by hand. Thus, an instantiation of the MicroBlaze soft-core processor and its additionally required IP cores (e.g. memory controller, data and code memories, . . .) were manually provided. Additionally, a simple IP core framework for the integration of the automatically generated VHDL source code of the SynDEVS model was provided.

Figure 4.7 depicts the atomic component of the UART serial line receiver. Two interesting points should be highlighted: First, how timing is implemented within the SynDEVS model in terms of the serial transmission protocol, and secondly, the readability and efficiency of the automatically generated synthesizable VHDL source code.

The timeout values of the StartBit, WaitForFirstBit, ReadBit, and Parity states directly represent the serial UART transmission protocol timing and will be detailed in the sequel. The Idle state is left over an external transition as soon as a logical 0 value is received on the serial receiver line RX (i.e. the beginning of the start bit). Then, the receiver stays within the StartBit state for 4.34 μs which is half the period of a serial bit. All other subsequent states responsible for receiving data, parity or stop bits will wait $8.68\mu s$ (i.e. the full period of a serial bit). Therefore, all subsequent bits are sampled approximately at the middle of the transmitted bit. This is necessary because the UART protocol does not include some dedicated clock signal and, thus, it has to be implemented self clocking. This means that the receiver synchronizes itself to the transmitter in terms of receiving a start signal. If during the waiting time of the start signal bit the logical value of the serial line jumps back to 1, an incomplete start bit was received and, thus, the receiver falls back into the Idle state. Otherwise, the receiver waits for a complete bit period (i.e. $8.68\mu s$) to receive the first bit of the transmitted eight bit data. Then, each bit of the eight bit data word is repeatedly read. Afterwards, the parity bit and the stop bit are read out. If both control bits were received successfully and the parity bit is correct, then, the received 8 bit data value is transmitted over the FSL master interface to the MicroBlaze soft-core processor.

Listing 4.1 depicts the transformation result of the ReadBit state. Please note that the complete synthesizable VHDL source code of the transformation result for the UART receiver model is included in Appendix A.3.

Listing 4.1 Transformation result for the ReadBit state of the UART receiver

```
74 when state_readbit =>
75   if (disable_in = '1' and TIMER=TO_UNSIGNED(0,timer_width) and
         rx_enable = '1' and (not (bitsread=TO_UNSIGNED(8,4)))) then
76     timer <= TO_UNSIGNED(867,10);
77     data <= rx&data(7 downto 1);
78     bitsread <= bitsread+TO_UNSIGNED(1,4);
79     evenparity <= rx xor evenparity;
80     state <= state_readbit;
81   end if;
82   if (disable_in = '1' and TIMER=TO_UNSIGNED(0,timer_width) and
         rx_enable = '1' and bitsread=TO_UNSIGNED(8,4)) then
83     timer <= TO_UNSIGNED(867,10);
84     evenparity <= rx xor evenparity;
85     state <= state_parity;
86   end if;
```

Within the transformation result, the original SynDEVS model's behaviour parts may be clearly identified. For instance, the variable assignments within a state are calculated whenever a transition into this state is executed. Thus, the variable assignments of the ReadBit state are only executed for the loop transition (i.e. $v_{Bits} \neq 8$), which is encoded by the first **if** statement. In contrast, the second **if** statement encodes the other internal transition leaving the ReadBit state to the Parity state. Within that **if** block, the variable assignments of the Parity state are executed. However, the transformation output is highly readable and, thus, expertise gained during the verification phase of the implementation (e.g. simulation of the circuit) may be easily reused to refine the original SynDEVS model.

Table 4.1 depicts a comparison of the resource usage and the estimated performance of the UART SynDEVS model against two UART IP cores written in VHDL and VeriLog. Both, the SynDEVS model and the FSL2Serial IP cores are implemented with FSL interfaces for receiving and transmitting data. The UartLite IP core does not contain FSL interfaces but a PLB[10] interface to the MicroBlaze processor. By looking at the resource utilization in terms of exploited registers, the SynDEVS model performs significantly better compared to the legacy IP cores. In contrast, the SynDEVS model utilize more LUTs than both other solutions. However, if the resource distribution is taken into account, which may be interpreted as a benchmark value regarding a good implementation perspective, the SynDEVS model performs negligible better than the other IP cores. The resource distribution is the number of used LUT[11] and register pairs and, thus, it is directly connected to the number of occupied FPGA slices after place and route. Thus, the IP core exploiting the automatically generated VHDL source code of the UART SynDEVS model performs best.

These results are a strong indicator that the described methodology for implementing the SynDEVS timing behaviour is highly efficient. The resources dedicated for UART data receiving and transmission are basically a

Table 4.1 Resource usage comparison of the automatically generated VHDL source code of a UART SynDEVS model against two different UART IP cores modelled in common hardware description languages

IP Core	Resource Utilization		Resource Distribution[b]	Performance[a] f_{max}
	Registers	LUTs		
SynDEVS model	86	173	184	294 MHz
FSL2Serial [Mar07]	102	160	187	293 MHz
UartLite [Xil11a]	148	133	206	297 MHz

[a] Timing numbers are only estimated after synthesis.
[b] Number of LUT and flip flop pairs used.

---

[10] *Processor Local Bus*
[11] *Lookup Table*

shift register clocked with the slow UART baud rate (i.e. approx. 115 KHz) and the exploited implementation methods among the other UART IP cores are almost the same. Thus, the variance within the different resource utilizations is dedicated to the implementation of the UART timing. All IP cores implement a fixed UART baud rate which has to be pre-defined before synthesis. However, the UartLite and FSL2Serial IP cores implement the baud rate setting by exploiting generic parameters. By doing so they include a delay counter with a large bit-width to deal with various kinds of baud rate and IP core clock rate combinations. In contrast, the transformation process for the SynDEVS UART model allocates only the smallest amount of bits needed for the timing register because, both, each states timeout value and the targeted clock rate, are given as an input to the described transformation process, cf. Section 4.2.2.

4.2.3 Optimization of Zero-Timeout States

States within SynDEVS models may be attributed with timeout values which split into three different classes: Zero-timeout (i.e. $\tau(s) = \{0\}$), real-timeout (i.e. $\tau(s) = \mathbb{R}^+ \setminus \{0, \infty\}$, and non-timeout (i.e. $\tau(s) = \{\infty\}$). Thus, the timing behaviour of SynDEVS components may be modelled with a fine granularity. The non-timeout value may be exploited to model the behaviour of traditional untimed state machines (e.g. Moore or Mealy machines). Real-timeout values are of utmost importance when modelling in the field of real-time or cyber-physical systems. Handling of time is an intrinsic property in such systems. However, the exploitation of zero-timeout states is highly beneficial when modelling control flow dominant systems. Specifically, the system behaviour is dynamically determined during runtime of the system by means of conditional execution.

Exploiting zero-timeout states within a SynDEVS model allows the designer to model complex conditional paths in which no time is passing by. Thus, the complex task of defining the conditional system behaviour is spread over a variety of model states which highly increases the readability and understandability of the model. Using zero-timeout state chains within SynDEVS model is comparable to exploiting variables within a VHDL process to sequentially describe a complex signal calculation. However, SynDEVS models with zero-timeout states impose high timing constraints on the implementation, cf. Section 4.2.2.

In [MSH11], the optimization algorithm depicted by Algorithm 4.2 was proposed to relocate the behaviour of zero-timeout state chains into adja-

Algorithm 4.2 State optimization algorithm for zero-timeout state chains

1 Identify all zero-timeout state chains
2 **for all** zero-timeout state chains **do**
3   Create state clusters (i.e. digraphs) for each start state of the chain
4 **end for**
5 **for all** state clusters **do**
6   Recursively traverse each cluster and relocate the state behaviour
    (i.e. output and variable assignments) into the non-zero-timeout state of
    the cluster
7   Rewrite internal and outgoing transitions of the cluster
8   Remove unused zero-timeout states and unused internal transitions
9 **end for**

cent non-zero-timeout states. This algorithm is being applied in the *Retiming* step of the proposed hardware / software co-design flow, cf. Figure 4.1.

Figure 4.8 depicts an example SynDEVS atomic component with zero-timeout states s_2, s_3, and s_4. The behaviour (i.e. variable and output port assignments) of these zero-timeout states may be relocated to the adjacent non-zero-timeout states s_0 and s_1 by applying Algorithm 4.2, which will be described in detail next. Thus, the resulting states s_0' and s_1', each including the behaviour of the zero-timeout states s_2, s_3, and s_4, will replace the original states s_0 and s_1, respectively.

During the first step of Algorithm 4.2, zero-timeout state chains are identified and marked. Purpose of the state marking is to identify possible start and end states of the zero-timeout state chains for the subsequent state clustering. Therefore, all zero-timeout states are initially marked with a distinct number. Then, a reachability graph is generated by passing the current state mark to all subsequently connected zero-timeout states (i.e. δ_{int}- or δ_{con}-reachable) until the state markings are not changed any more. Additionally, all traversed transitions, which are used during the reachability graph generation, are marked as well. Please note that during the state marking, the precondition for a zero-timeout chain (i.e. cycle free) is checked by verifying that a state was not marked before with that specific mark. Additionally, it is checked that no external transition is linked to a state within the zero-timeout state chain.

State clusters are created at step 3 of Algorithm 4.2. For each start state of a zero-timeout state chain a separate cluster is created which contain

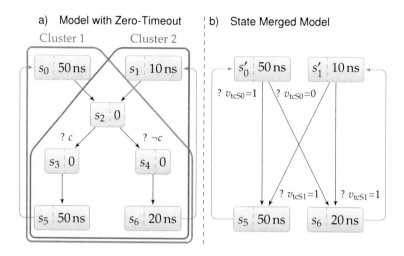

Figure 4.8 Example SynDEVS atomic component a) before and b) after state behaviour relocation [MSH11]

all reachable states (i.e. the zero-timeout states from the chain and the finally reached non-zero-timeout states). Thus, a state may be a member of different clusters (e.g. two zero-timeout state chains ending in the same final state or two state chains which are joined together at some inner state). The clusters are represented as digraphs with a simple structure: They have a single non-zero-timeout start state and one or more end states which are non-zero-timeout states, too. In between these non-zero-timeout states are the states of the zero-timeout state chains only. The edges connecting the states of the digraph represent the δ_{int} or δ_{con} transitions. Thus, if a state of the digraph has multiple successor or ancestor states, the edges are annotated with the conditions of the original transitions which led to that path. For instance, there are two clusters depicted in Figure 4.8. The first cluster starts at state s_0 and ends at the final states s_5 and s_6 including the inner zero-timeout states s_2, s_3, and s_4. In contrast, the second cluster starts at state s_1 but the rest of the cluster is equivalent to the first one.

After the state clusters are created, the state behaviour of the zero-timeout states are relocated in step 6 of Algorithm 4.2. Each cluster is independently optimized. Basically, all variable and output port assignments of the inner zero-timeout states are relocated to the start state (i.e. a non-zero-timeout state) of the digraph. However, this behaviour relocation

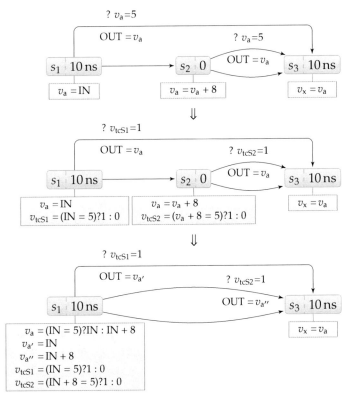

Figure 4.9 Example of the recursive state behaviour relocation

involves a critical task regarding the assignments: Different conditional paths may lead to different assignments and state traversal. Thus, temporary variables are introduced to mark the traversed zero-timeout path. Based upon these variables, new transitions may be created to reconstruct the original behaviour of the original unoptimized model.

On the left side of Figure 4.8, the state s_2 is conditionally linked to either state s_3 or s_4. Therefore, during the optimization step of each cluster, a temporary variable describing the traversed path is introduced: v_{tcS0} for Cluster 1 and v_{tcS1} for Cluster 2. These temporary variables will be set in the states s_0' and s_1' depending on the old transition condition c and, thus, they describe on which path the original model would be traversed. Based on this evaluation the correct internal transition to the states s_5 or s_6 could be taken. Thus, the optimized model reassembles the behaviour of the original model.

Figure 4.9 depicts these recursive behaviour relocation steps and temporary variable introduction in detail. The top part of the figure shows the initial digraph with start state s_1 and a single final state s_3. The middle part depicts the introduced temporary variables v_{tcS1} and v_{tcS2} which mark the different traversal paths through the digraph. For instance, the assignment of v_{tcS1} is

$$v_{tcS1} = (IN = 5)?1 : 0.$$

Thus, v_{tcS1} will be set to 1 if $IN = 5$ holds true, otherwise it will be set to 0. Please note that during this step, the transition conditions are rewritten to exploit the newly introduced temporary variables. The bottom part of Figure 4.9 shows the digraph after the complete state behaviour relocation. The complete assignments from state s_2 are relocated to s_1. During the recursive relocation, the occurrence of a variable inside an assignment is replaced by the evaluated variable value. Therefore, the original assignment from v_a of state s_1 is renamed to $v_{a'}$ and from state s_2 to $v_{a''}$. To sustain the original model behaviour, the variable v_a is assigned to either $v_{a'}$ or $v_{a''}$ depending on the traversed path (i.e. conditionally assigned). However, $v_{a'}$, $v_{a''}$, and v_{tcS1} may not be used directly within the assignment because all variables are assigned concurrently within a state. Thus, the new assignment of v_a is

$$v_a = \underbrace{(IN = 5)?}_{:= v_{tcS1}} \underbrace{IN}_{:= v_{a'}} : \underbrace{IN + 8}_{:= v_{a''}} .$$

The possible duplication of evaluation terms is the downside of the described approach. In theory, the generated terms for the temporary variables could be further optimized. For instance, introduced but unused variables could be removed and partial evaluation of the conditional assignments could further optimize the assignment terms. However, these low-level optimization is postponed to the subsequent design-flow steps after the SynDEVS to VHDL transformation and, thus, the exploited VHDL synthesis tool (i.e. Xilinx XST [Xil09b]) will perform logic reduction and duplicate register removal. The results of the application example in Section 6.1.3 depict that the resource utilization after synthesis of both, an unoptimized and an optimized model, is at least equivalent. Thus, the presented optimization algorithm solely optimizes the timing behaviour without any inappropriate impacts on resource utilization.

4.2.4 Back-Annotation of Resource Utilization

After a successful synthesis run of a SynDEVS model, the resource usage may be back-annotated to the original SynDEVS model. The resource usage on an IP core level (i.e. the entire resource utilization of a transformed SynDEVS model) can inartifically be obtained from the synthesis informational log messages. However, retrieving the resource usage of a SynDEVS model with fine granularity (e.g. resources for state space encoding or timeout handling) is complicated but of utmost importance for the model designer. Based on these extracted figures of merit, the designer may refine the model to reach the design requirements. For instance, an atomic component including a high resource utilization within the variable assignments could be split into different components to allow resource sharing. Thus, back-annotation of the resource utilization is a foundation for implementing more sophisticated optimization algorithms to (semi-) automatically perform scheduling and partitioning (e.g. [YWH^{+}10]) or in general design exploration methodologies (e.g. [YHS10, WRZ^{+}11]), just to name a few.

Back-annotation of the resource utilization with fine granularity requires a direct analysis of the synthesis output for the transformed SynDEVS model (i.e. the netlist which is synthesized for the generated VHDL source code). Thus, the back-annotation method described later on is tailored to the exploited synthesis tool (i.e. Xilinx EDK[12] which is part of the Xilinx ISE[13] Design Suite) but may be applicable to other synthesis tools as well. The Xilinx EDK tool-suite synthesizes each IP core (i.e. each transformed SynDEVS model) into a single *.ngc* file which is basically a binary but proprietary netlist file format. However, they supply a tool for transforming the *.ngc* file into an *.edif* file which stores the netlist in the vendor-neutral file format EDIF[14]. Based upon this netlist file format, the back-annotation of the resource usage is implemented. Listing 4.3 illustrates such an EDIF netlist.

Listing 4.3 Example of a netlist file in Electronic Design Interchange Format (EDIF)

```
1 (edif devs_uart_0_wrapper (edifVersion 2 0 0)
2   (edifLevel 0) (keywordMap (keywordLevel 0))
3   (status (written (timestamp 2010 11 18 17 26 24)
```

---

[12] *Embedded Development Kit*

[13] *Integrated Synthesis Environment*

[14] *Electronic Design Interchange Format*

```
4      (program "Xilinx_ngc2edif" (version "M.70d"))
5        ...
6    )
7    (external UNISIMS
8      (edifLevel 0) (technology (numberDefinition))
9      (cell LUT4
10       (cellType GENERIC)
11         (view view_1
12           (viewType NETLIST)
13           (interface
14             (port I0 (direction INPUT))
15               ...
16   )))
17     ....
18   )
19   (library devs_uart_0_wrapper_lib
20     (edifLevel 0) (technology (numberDefinition))
21     (cell devs_uart_0_wrapper
22       (cellType GENERIC)
23         (view view_1
24           (viewType NETLIST)
25           (interface
26             (port Clk (direction INPUT))
27             (port (array (rename FSL_M_Data "FSL_M_Data<0:31>") 32)
                    (direction OUTPUT))
28               ...
29             (designator "xc5vlx110tff1136-1")
30           )
31           (contents
32             (instance (rename devs_uart_0_UART_INSTANCE_TRANSM...
                    ITTER_MAP_state_FSM_FFd2_renamed_2
33                 "devs_uart_0/UART_INSTANCE/TRANSMITTER_MAP/
                    state_FSM_FFd2")
34               (viewRef view_1 (cellRef FDC (libraryRef UNISIMS)))
35               (property XSTLIB (boolean (true)) (owner "Xilinx"))
36               (property INIT (string "0") (owner "Xilinx"))
37             )
38               ...
39           )
40   ))))
```

The Xilinx EDK IP core which exploits the generated VHDL source code of
the SynDEVS model is included as a *library* at line 19. Within that block,
all utilized resources are embedded as *instance*s with a reference to the
exploited Xilinx FPGA resource at line 34. Thus, by analysing the *instance*
name, it can be deduced that the state encoding of the atomic component
named *TRANSMITTER* instantiate a *FDC* cell (i.e. a flip-flop).

The *instance* name describes both, the SynDEVS component and the component part utilizing the resource. Identifying the part is only possible because of the regular structure of the generated VHDL source code. For instance, all state timeout related arithmetic is implemented through the use of a single timer VHDL signal. After synthesis, the generated netlist includes cell instances with the name ... _MAP_timer... which reflect the arithmetic expressions of the timer register as well as the timer register itself. Even more, all register and logic cells related to the state encoding have ... _state_ ... inside their instance names. Thus, by analysing the instance name it is possible to back-annotate the resource utilization to the following component parts: Output ports, variables, states, state timeout handling, and temporary variables introduced by the zero-state aggregation. However, identifying the correct part of an instance name which is related to a component part is a tedious task because the EDIF instance names include much more information. Thus, each instance name has to be mapped against regular expressions to filter out irrelevant parts of the name. For example, the remainder of an instance name of a port or variable may be detected by the following regular expression depicted by Listing 4.4.

Listing 4.4 Regular expression to detect the remainder of an instance name for a variable or port

```
1 (_[0-9]+|_enable|_(mult|mux|xor|xnor|and|or|not|cmp|sub|add|addsub|
     cmp_eq|cmp_lt|cmp_gt|cmp_ge|share)[0-9]*|<[0-9]+>[0-9]*|_wg|_(cy
     |share|wg|sw|rt|inv|lut|f|g|rstpot)[0-9]*)+
```

As the vendor of the exploited synthesis tool does not describe the relation between the generated instance names and the VHDL source code input, this regular expression as well as other regular expressions to map the different instance names to the component parts were built by trial and error. Every time the back-annotation is performed and an unknown instance name is detected the expressions have to be extended accordingly. Thus, these regular expressions are tailored to the specific synthesis tool and exploited target platform (i.e. Xilinx Virtex-5 FPGA) and are likely not complete for all the others possible FPGA target architectures.

All resources are back-annotated heuristically to the SynDEVS model by the following method: For the first part of the instance name, the related SynDEVS atomic or parallel component will be identified within the model. Afterwards, for the unparsed rest of the instance name (i.e. without the part identifying the component) it will be expected that it is reflecting either an output port, variable assignment, temporary variable assignment, state, or state timeout part. Thus, it is matched against regular expressions built for these parts. If it matches, the cell referenced by the instance will be added as an exploited resource to the SynDEVS model.

After applying the back-annotation, the SynDEVS model includes the following fine granular resource usage information: Each component is annotated with the resource usage in terms of registers and LUTs of itself and all sub-components. The resource usage of each atomic component is split into the following different parts:

Output ports: Resources to assign the output ports event values.

Variables: Resources to store the variable values and to calculate the variable assignments annotated to a state.

Temporary variables: Resources which are introduced by the optimization method to remove zero-timeout state chains. This resources usage is not annotated to the component but to the non-zero-timeout state introducing the overhead.

States: Resources introduced by the VHDL FSM to encode the SynDEVS states. This consumption heavily depends on the FSM implementation strategy (e.g. one-hot encoding or Gray code) of the synthesis tool.

State timeout handling: Resources which are introduced by the described methodology of implementing the state timeouts in terms of a timer register.

These resource usage informations are embedded within the original SynDEVS model and may be viewed by using the GUI described in Chapter 5. Even more, these annotations could be exploited by optimization tools for automated model refinement which are not part of this work and, thus, this topic is not further discussed. However, they are at least of some importance for the designer to optimize the SynDEVS model and for deriving the hardware and software partitioning to be exploited during the hardware / software co-design.

4.3 SynDEVS to Software Transformation

In order to execute SynDEVS model in software, two fundamentally different methodologies may be exploited. First, the SynDEVS model may be transformed to software exploiting a general purpose processor and, secondly, it may transformed to run on a special purpose processor. In the following, both approaches are discussed in detail.

Running a SynDEVS model as software on a general purpose processor is very beneficial in terms of compatibility with legacy source code. Usually, general purpose processors feature a large set of compilers for various programming languages and, thus, a programming language may be chosen which match available legacy or proprietary source code libraries. In contrast, software running on a special purpose processor will not integrate well with other source code libraries and, thus, once gained expertise may be lost. However, such a processor would execute Syn-DEVS models very efficiently in terms of resource usage and execution speed but the processor instruction set has to be chosen carefully to execute SynDEVS models (e.g. introduce special instructions for state timeout handling). Thus, execution of generic, legacy software libraries would be only possible with a high effort, if it is feasible at all with the chosen instruction set of the special purpose processor. Either the legacy software libraries have to be completely rewritten as SynDEVS models or a new compiler has to be developed to cross-compile the legacy software libraries to the limited instruction set of the special purpose processor. However, a SynDEVS-related special purpose processor would be appropriate in terms of timeout handling because time would be an inherent property of both, the processor and the software running on it. Usually, common software programming languages (e.g. Java or C) cannot express time directly. Thus, a substantial overhead will be introduced to proper handle state timeouts with traditional programming languages. In contrast, a special purpose processor may handle state timeouts without such a downside and, thus, the smallest possible state timeout value which may be expressed by a Syn-DEVS model will be lower on a special purpose processor compared to a general purpose processor.

The main goal of running a SynDEVS model as software is to allow interfacing with legacy software written in common software programming languages. Thus, software execution on a general purpose processor was chosen over implementing a special purpose processor for SynDEVS model execution. By doing so, a stock compiler may be used to compile legacy software. However, for each exploited target platform (e.g. Xilinx MicroBlaze) a support library has to be developed to allow proper state timeout handling. Additionally, a model-to-text transformation from Syn-DEVS models to each exploited source code language has to be defined. As most embedded systems development platforms feature a C/C++ compiler, a transformation from SynDEVS to C++ is proposed in [MKH12], which will be detailed next.

4.3.1 SynDEVS MoC to C++ Transformation

A low memory footprint is one of embedded systems most important properties because of tight resource constraints. However, C++ may not feature a low memory footprint if certain languages constructs are exploited (e.g. overloading *virtual* class functions may result in large vtables). Thus, the subset of C++ has to be chosen carefully but exploitation of the object-oriented approach from C++ is very beneficial regarding readability of the transformation output. Another advantage is that, both, legacy C and C++ source code libraries, may be reused within SynDEVS models.

The SynDEVS to C++ transformation process is comparable to the transformation methodology exploited for SynDEVS to VHDL transformation, cf. Section 4.2.2. Thus, the basic concepts regarding state timeout implementation (i.e. τ_{gcd} calculation) and readability of the transformation output (i.e. C++ source code) are exploited for the software transformation, too. Therefore, only the differences of the SynDEVS to C++ transformation compared to the SynDEVS to VHDL transformation are discussed in the following sections.

The SynDEVS to C++ transformation process is split into four different parts. First, for each target platform, a SynDEVS software support library has to be developed to implement the state timeout handling. This step must be done only once for each exploited platform. Second, the behaviour of SynDEVS models has to be transformed into C++. A suitable model execution process must be defined to run the concurrent SynDEVS models sequentially on the target platform. Thirdly, a special type of SynDEVS component needs to be introduced to allow an easy integration of legacy software libraries into SynDEVS. Finally, events must be distributed within the different SynDEVS components running in software or hardware. Thus, the communication interfaces in between hardware and software components has to be generated automatically.

Software Support Library

Figure 4.10 depicts the introduced SynDEVS MoC software support library classes as well as the essential classes of a SynDEVS model. The classes

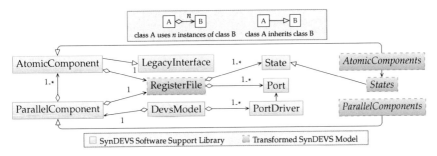

Figure 4.10 UML class diagram of SynDEVS MoC transformation into C++ source code [MKH12]

drawn with a solid border are (abstract) base classes of the SynDEVS Software Support Library. They are the foundation for executing SynDEVS MoC in real-time. The dashed border classes will be generated during the transformation process. The SynDEVS model's components, states, variables, ports, and connections will be transformed into classes inheriting these base classes.

The *DevsModel* class manages the execution of the SynDEVS model and, thus, handles the behaviour of the model, which will be described later on in more detail. Both, the *Port* and *PortDriver* class handle the communication between software and hardware parts. As the communication strongly depends upon the exploited target platform, the communication handling is split into these two classes with each having a different abstraction level. The *PortDriver* class is a pure abstract class which must be detailed for each exploited communication type (e.g. FSL). Thus, it implements the communication on a low hardware level. In contrast, the *Port* class handles the communication on the abstract MoC level. Thus, independently of the exploited communication type, it provides an interface for sending or receiving a SynDEVS event. The *ParallelComponent* class is an abstract base class for implementing SynDEVS parallel components. Thus, it encapsulates all parallel or atomic sub-components and handles the event distribution between them through the input and output ports. The *AtomicComponent* class is an abstract base class aimed to control the behaviour execution of SynDEVS MoCs. Thus, this class provides basic functionality for updating the model status (e.g. change current model state or execute transition functions). These functions will be called by the *DevsModel* class at each evaluation cycle. This class orchestrates the interaction of all the

Figure 4.11 Hardware / software architecture of SynDEVS MoC exploiting a Xilinx MicroBlaze soft-core processor [MKH12]

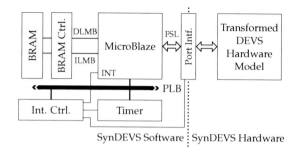

different parts. For instance, when an incoming event (e.g. an event received over the communication link from the hardware part) is detected, the toplevel parallel component will be informed about that event and, subsequently, it will be distributed to the atomic component connected to its toplevel input port. Then, the external transition is executed changing the current SynDEVS model state and a new state timeout value is registered. Thus, the *DevsModel* class is triggered at each SynDEVS model evaluation cycle ensuring that all events are distributed, handled, and new timeout values are considered.

While most of these software support library classes are generic and independent of the exploited target platform, some are tailored to it. Specifically, the *DevsModel* and *PortDriver* class are strictly related to the target architecture and must be provided for each exploited platform. The presented transformation methodology was implemented for a Xilinx MicroBlaze soft-core processor target platform as a proof of concept.

Target Platform

Figure 4.11 depicts the hardware / software architecture of a SynDEVS model exploiting a Xilinx MicroBlaze soft-core processor. Please note that Figure 4.11 features a single MicroBlaze for simplicity only. The described methodology is not limited to a single hardware or software instance and, thus, multiple instances may be exploited. The MicroBlaze processor executes the SynDEVS model software parts generated by the transformation of SynDEVS MoC to C++ source code. The model's hardware part is connected by exploiting a FSL link. A thin communication interface layer in between the software and hardware part is automatically generated and described later on in more detail. However, the *PortDriver* class reflects the software part of the communication interface and, thus, it has to be provided for each exploited communication method. Please note that additional communication methods (e.g. a bus or shared memory communication) may be easily introduced as the SynDEVS model does not explicitly specify the communication type or structure.

State timeouts are implemented by exploiting a programmable timer IP core (i.e. Xilinx xps_timer [Xil10b]) which is connected to the MicroBlaze through an interrupt controller. Whenever a state timeout occurs, the interrupt controller issues an interrupt request to the MicroBlaze processor to start executing a single SynDEVS model execution cycle. Additionally, an incoming SynDEVS event from the model's hardware part will issue an interrupt request, too. Therefore, the port interface communication layer is connected to an interrupt controller (i.e. Xilinx xps_intc [Xil10a]) in addition to the timer IP core. The *DevsModel* class heavily depends on the exploited target platform. For instance, each atomic component will register its current state timeout at the *DevsModel* class. Thus, the timer IP core must be programmed accordingly to achieve the requested timeout. Additionally, a platform-specific interrupt service routine has to be provided for the exploited platform to detect if a confluent transition has to be executed in case of an interrupt request spawned at the same point in time by an incoming SynDEVS event and a state timeout event.

Model Behaviour Transformation

Each atomic component from the SynDEVS model is represented by its own child class of `AtomicComponents`. The base class provides some basic functionality to inform the `DevsModel` (i.e. the instance which executes the behaviour), about its current state and state timeout in τ_{gcd} steps. Thus, the source code of each component's child class only reflect its own behaviour. The execution of an atomic component's class is orchestrated by the `DevsModel` class together with the `AtomicComponents` base class.

However, each state of an atomic component is implemented as a child class of `State`. In contrast, these state classes are only storing information (i.e. a state identifier and the state timeout) but do not provide any additional functionality. Thus, they are implemented as **const** classes which have a considerably lower memory footprint compared to normal classes with function inheritance. Listing 4.5 depicts such a state definition.

Listing 4.5 Example of a state definition

```
35 class ComponentState_transmitter_sendbit : public ComponentState {
36 public:
37   ComponentState_transmitter_sendbit() _CONST_INIT_SECTION:
        ComponentState(STATE_transmitter_SENDBIT,0)  {};
38 };
```

Within the atomic component class, each state is instantiated together with the input ports, output ports, and variables. Listing 4.6 depicts the class definition of such a transformed atomic component.

Listing 4.6 Example of an atomic component definition

```
60 class Atomic_Component_transmitter : public Atomic_Component {
61 public:
62   Atomic_Component_transmitter() _CONST_INIT_SECTION :
63       Atomic_Component(&registerFile.currentState_transmitter),
64       variable_send(&registerFile.variable_transmitter_send),
65       variable_parity(&registerFile.variable_transmitter_parity),
66       variable_bits(&registerFile.variable_transmitter_bits),
67       variable_transmit(&registerFile.variable_transmitter_transmit)
68       { };
69   void reset() const; //override
70   void eventRun() const; //override
71   // Output Ports
72   static Port1Bit* const outport_dataack;
73   static Port1Bit* const outport_tx;
74   // Input Ports
75   static PortU8Bit* const inport_data;
76   // Variables
77   int32_t* const variable_send;
78   int32_t* const variable_parity;
79   int32_t* const variable_bits;
80   int32_t* const variable_transmit;
81 private:
82   // States
83   ComponentState_transmitter_idle const state_idle;
84   ComponentState_transmitter_readdata const state_readdata;
85   ComponentState_transmitter_sendbit const state_sendbit;
86   ComponentState_transmitter_sendparity const state_sendparity;
87   ComponentState_transmitter_init const state_init;
88   ComponentState_transmitter_stopbit const state_stopbit;
89   ComponentState_transmitter_startbit const state_startbit;
90 };
```

All data fields (i.e. input ports, output ports, and variables) are not directly instantiated within the atomic component's class. It is centrally stored at a register file and, thus, only pointers to the register file are instantiated as place holders for the data. By doing so, the generated executable file will have different sections for code and data. Even more, code and data sections may be split into generic data and code required to execute a SynDEVS model and into model specific data and code sections. Thus, an embedded system may exploit different memory types for storing these informations. For instance, the generic code may be stored in a non-volatile ROM but the SynDEVS model code section may be stored inside a volatile ROM (i.e. E^2PROM). Please note that these register file pointers are **const** and are initialized outside the constructor's body as member variables. Thus, the storage location (i.e. value of the pointer) is known at compile time and may be optimized by the compiler. This approach is highly memory and runtime efficient because the value of input and output events are directly stored within the register file without any complex dereferencing at execution time.

The atomic component child classes have to override the base class functions `reset()` and `eventRun()` to implement the model behaviour. Within the `reset()` function the component is initialised into its initial state and initial values of the variables are set, cf. Listing 4.7.

Listing 4.7 Example of an atomic component's initialisation function

```
3  void  Atomic_Component_transmitter :: reset ()  const  {
4      //  Outport  init
5      this –>outport_dataack –>data =0;
6      this –>outport_dataack –>isActive=false ;
7      this –>outport_tx –>data =0;
8      this –>outport_tx –>isActive=false ;
9      //  Variable  initialization
10     *variable_send  =  0;
11     *variable_parity  =  0;
12     *variable_bits  =  0;
13     *variable_transmit  =  0;
14     //  Set  Initial  State
15     startNewState (( ComponentState  *  const )  &state_init );
16 }
```

The `eventRun()` function implements the executable behaviour (i.e. state transitions and variable and port assignments). Listing 4.8 depicts the transformation result for a state with an external transition and assignment of variables.

Listing 4.8 Example of an atomic component's state behaviour implementation

```
38   case STATE_transmitter_READDATA:{ //=state_readdata
39     if (this->current_state->current_time == 0) {
40       this->outport_dataack->data = 1;
41       this->outport_dataack->isActive = true;
42       this->outport_tx->data = (*variable_transmit);
43       this->outport_tx->isActive = true;
44       register int tempVariable_send = (0<<7 | (*variable_send>>1 &
               127));
45       register int tempVariable_parity = (*variable_send>>0 & 1);
46       register int tempVariable_transmit = (*variable_send>>0 & 1);
47       *variable_send = tempVariable_send;
48       *variable_parity = tempVariable_parity;
49       *variable_transmit = tempVariable_transmit;
50       startNewState((ComponentState * const) &state_startbit);
51     }
52     break;
53   }
```

To implement the required concurrent assignment of variables, all assignments are evaluated into temporary variables first and afterwards, assigned to the target variable within the register file. Please note that all pointer dereferences (e.g. **this**->inport_data->isActive or *variable_-send) are constant and known at compile time. Thus, the runtime complexity of these constructs are equal to a direct memory read or write operation with a fixed address. Therefore, these data access operations are commonly executed within a single processor cycle but are highly readable compared to a direct memory location access. Appendix A.4 depicts the complete example source code of an atomic component implementing an UART transceiver.

Model Execution

Embedded systems processors usually exploit only single-core architectures and, thus, software execution of the concurrent SynDEVS models transformed C++ source code is a sequential process. In the following, the approach to emulate the parallel behaviour on a single-core architecture is described.[15] The execution of SynDEVS models transformed to C++ source code mimic the execution methodology of concurrent behaviour exploited in hardware simulators or concurrent programming languages (e.g. VHDL

---

[15] Please note that multi-core architectures may be targeted, too. Hence, this approach would require preliminary allocation and scheduling assignments (e.g. [YWH+10]) not covered here.

or SystemC).

The SynDEVS model components are evaluated by the following evaluation cycle.

1. *Schedule input events:* All model input events are read and scheduled for processing by passing them to the atomic components.

2. *Sequential execution:* Atomic components are sequentially executed in indeterministic order. However, only the atomic components will be executed which are activated due to input events or due to a timeout event.

3. *Evaluate model:* The model behaviour will be executed. Thus, the output events are evaluated and the next state of the atomic components are registered.

4. *Emit output events:* Emit all output events and activate the next state of each component (e.g. register the new state timeout value at the programmable timer IP core). Return to Step 1.

Each instance of the SynDEVS model may have its own local discrete clock cycle. Thus, the model behaviour (e.g. variable assignments or legacy code execution) has to be computable within such a clock dependent period. However, this period may vary within different target architectures. For instance, the MicroBlaze-based target platform, introduced in Section 4.3.1, is running at 125 MHz. Thus, the discrete clock period is approx. 2.9 µs: 139 clock cycles are required to handle the interrupt request for state timeouts. Additionally, 220 clock cycles are required to activate and execute the behaviour of a single, basic atomic component (i.e. a component which emits a received single input event back to the sender).

Event Distribution

Parallel components are elaborated during the transformation phase and, thus, all port connections are dissolved in terms of using a register file. This means that the emitted output ports event values are stored centrally at a register file and all events are distributed in situ within the same software instances. An additional flag is stored besides the event value which denotes the port's state (i.e. if an event occurred within the evaluation cycle). All input ports connected to the same output port will point to the same specific register file location. Thus, whenever an input port is exploited, the current value of the output port will be directly used in terms of a constant pointer dereferencing to the current output port's event value. However, to avoid indeterministic behaviour, both output port's event values, the current one and the new to be emitted value, must be stored separately. Then, the new event value of the output port will replace the current value after finishing the current evaluation cycle. By doing so, independently of the sequential execution order of different concurrent components, each component will exploit the valid event value, regardless if the port is emitting a new event. This behaviour is comparable to concurrent signal assignments within VHDL sequential process blocks.

Events in between different instances (i.e. either between software instances or software and hardware instance) must be appropriately distributed. Such a distribution channel is mainly defined by the exploited target platform and, therefore, for each exploited platform an automatic interface generation must be supplied by the transformation process. The MicroBlaze-based target platform use FSL for communication between the instances, cf. Figure 4.11, which will be detailed in Section 4.3.2. However, other common inter-process or multi-core communication methods (e.g. shared-memory or bus) may be exploited as well.

Regardless of the exploited communication method, it is of utmost importance that the causality chain of event transmission and reception is kept intact. Thus, if event e_1 is transmitted before event e_2, then e_1 has to be received and evaluated at the receiving atomic component before event e_2. However, this property may not hold true for some communication method implementations. For instance, a communication method may involve an arbiter which reorders bus data within a certain amount of time to minimize latency (e.g. [PNA+11]) or power consumption (e.g. [CN01]).

Another important aspect of the exploited communication method is the congestion handling. Congestion may arise if one component generates events faster than the receiving component may consume. This case may easily come up if during component generation the events are placed inside hardware while the consumer component is implemented as software. However, the different components may be evaluated regarding their emit and receive rates due to their annotated state timeout values. Thus, one of SynDEVS main advantages, namely the annotation and consideration of time, becomes visible. In respect of the different state timeout values, the designer is able to decide on the model software and hardware partitioning (i.e. which SynDEVS model components should be run on a slow instance or a fast one).

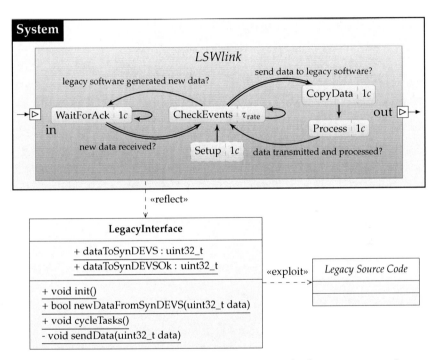

Figure 4.12 Dedicated *LSWlink* SynDEVS component for legacy source code reuse support. The behaviour of the SynDEVS states are enriched by calls to the LegacyInterface class which acts as a middleware in between the SynDEVS model and the legacy source code library. Data exchange is handled solely by the SynDEVS atomic component intrinsic variables.

Embedding Legacy C/C++ Source Code

The reuse of available legacy C/C++ source code is mandatory for increasing the acceptance of modelling complex systems by exploiting MoCs. Following a best practice approach, MoCs may be utilized for newly created system parts but reuse existing legacy source code for the rest of the system. Basically, legacy C/C++ source code usage within a MoC can be split into the following four basic phases:

1. *Setup:* Initialize the legacy software library.

2. *Send request:* Transfer data from MoC to software.

3. *Process:* Execute software to start the processing of the transferred data.

4. *Get result:* Transfer processed data from software back to MoC.

Some of these phases may be skipped with respect to the use case of the exploited legacy source code library. For instance, a component solely consuming events (e.g. legacy source code driver to output audio data) may skip the last phase (i.e. transfer result back to MoC).

A special type of atomic SynDEVS component named *LSWlink* is proposed to ease the integration of legacy software libraries. While the overall behaviour of the component is completely denoted as a SynDEVS component, cf. Figure 4.12, the behaviour of the single states are enriched by calls to the legacy source code library executed as software. For this purpose, the transformation process provides a generic C++ interface class `LegacyInterface`, which contains methods to reflect all four phases as given above. Thus, to employ legacy source code within a SynDEVS model, the dedicated *LSWlink* component has only to be copied to the SynDEVS model of the system. Then, the transformation process automatically generates the required `LegacyInterface` class. However, the designer has to provide the interfacing to the legacy source code library in terms of declaring the behaviour of the functions of this middleware class by hand.

Data exchange between the legacy source code and the SynDEVS model is handled solely by the intrinsic variables of the SynDEVS atomic component. Whenever an input event is received, the CopyData state stores the input event value inside a variable. Afterwards, within the Process state, the `LegacyComponent` method to process the data is executed. If the process has to transfer data back to the SynDEVS model, the resulting data has to be stored inside a variable, too. Afterwards, this variable's data is emitted over an output port of the SynDEVS model *LSWlink* component.

The annotated state timeout value of the CheckEvents state ensures that the legacy software library will be polled periodically for new data. The timeout value τ_{rate} may be set to an arbitrary value suitable for the use case. However, the exploited target architecture running the software must be capable of handling the defined period τ_{rate} (e.g. greater than $2.9\mu s$ at the proposed MicroBlaze-based architecture). Please note that the timeout values of other states are set to $1c$ (i.e. one τ_{gcd} clock period), which denotes the smallest achievable discrete time step on the target architecture and, thus, no specific value is given in the generic *LSWlink* component.

4.3.2 Communication Interface Generation

Implementing a SynDEVS model with components tailored to software and hardware instances requires a communication interface generation between the different instance types. The communication interface type depends both, on the targeted platform architecture and on the type of instances, which should be connected. Thus, connecting two different hardware instances (e.g. SynDEVS model parts implemented on different FPGAs) may be easily achieved by defining a communication interface which exploits the plain IO pins of the FPGA: Each port requires $n + 1$ pins where n is the bit-width of the event value data type and an additional dedicated pin to carry an enable signal of the port (i.e. notify target about the occurrence of a port event). In contrast, connecting two software instances or a software instance to a hardware instance requires a more sophisticated communication interface which has to fit the exploited processor executing the software SynDEVS model. Many communication schemes exist for connecting different processors or processors with coprocessors. The most prominent ones are bus, shared-memory, and point-to-point connections.

A bus-driven connection of the different SynDEVS hardware and software parts is highly appreciated if no static connections between the different components exists. Thus, RecDEVS exploits a bus communication scheme because each dynamically reconfigured component may communicate to each other. Hence, such a degree of freedom regarding the interconnect of components comes with high implementation costs to avoid bus congestion. For each model it has to be deduced how many events may be transmitted over the bus within a single discrete time step. Then, the bus has to be implemented with such an event storage capacity [MWH10].

A shared-memory based interconnect is highly appreciated when a large amount of data should be preserved for some time or will occur at the same time. However, a shared-memory may have congestion issues, too. To connect n components to the memory without congestion, it needs to be clocked very fast to multiplex the access of n components within a single discrete time step.

Point-to-point connections may be exploited if the connections between the components are static. Then, a congestion free communication is possible without great impact on implementation costs because no complex communication interface (e.g. a bus arbiter) needs to be implemented. However, it does not scale very well if each component needs to communicate with each other because the amount of point-to-point links for n components is $K_n = \binom{n-1}{2}$, cf. complete graphs in [GS93, p. 463].

The MicroBlaze processor exploited for the SynDEVS models software parts is capable of implementing all three communication schemes. For a bus based communication, the PLB may be exploited, hence it cannot handle multiple, parallel data transfers between different components. Thus, it may not be used within SynDEVS because of the risk of congestion which would render event transmissions indeterministic. A shared-memory may be connected to the processor through PLB or LMB[16] memory controllers. However, BRAMs[17] available at the exploited Virtex-5 FPGA have only a dual-port access scheme and a true multi-port memory for n components may only be implemented by exploiting advanced memory access methods (e.g. multi-pumping or BRAM replication [LS10]) which come with additional implementation costs. In contrast, a point-to-point connection may be implemented with the MicroBlaze processor through FSL. Using FSL requires only a basic interface and, thus, it is very lightweight and comes with almost no additional implementation costs. Even more, a 32-bit data transfer over the FSL will only take a single processor cycle and is congestion free. However, each MicroBlaze processor may utilize a maximum of 32 FSL connections where each FSL connection is only uni-directional. Hence, it perfectly fit the communication interface requirements (i.e. deterministic behaviour, congestion free, and lightweight implementation) for connecting a dozen of components where only a couple of components need to communicate with each other.

In the following, the automated generation of a FSL interface in between the SynDEVS software and hardware parts is described, cf. *Port Intf.* depicted in Figure 4.11. First, an overview of how to transmit SynDEVS events

---

[16] *Local Memory Bus*
[17] *Block RAMs*

over such a fixed bit-width communication interface is given. Second, the automatic generation of the communication interface is detailed.

Mapping of SynDEVS Ports

Different possibilities of mapping SynDEVS ports from a hardware instance to a software instance exist. Because the targeted processor of SynDEVS software models is a MicroBlaze processor, it will be discussed, how to map SynDEVS ports of an arbitrary bit-widths to a fixed 32 bit-width communication interface (i.e. FSL).

The FSL communication interface is uni-directional and, thus, a single FSL interface is exploited for all input ports and another one for all output ports. In the following, only *ports* are discussed without going into greater detail if either input or output ports are mapped.

Parallel Let assume that

p_i $\in$ P are the ports which should be mapped between both instances

n $=$ $|P|$ is the number of ports

$|p_i|$ $\in$ $\mathbb{N}$ is the bit-width of the ports p_i event value data type.

Then, the overall amount of bits m to be mapped between both instances is:

$$m = n + \sum_{i=1}^{n} |p_i| \, .$$

Therefore, if the exploited communication interface bit-with is smaller or equal m, the ports may be directly mapped in parallel to the data words transferred over the communication link. For instance, a single 31 bit-width port may be mapped directly to a FSL data word or 16 single bit ports may be mapped, too. However, if m exceed the communication interface bit-with further serialization of the event values to be transmitted has to be introduced.

Split A basic method is the split and merge of ports. Then, the data words to be transmitted will be split into junks of 32 bits. Thus, $\lceil \frac{m}{32} \rceil$ FSL data words have to be transmitted. In hardware, the split and merge of data words may be described by basic VHDL signal vector array operations (e.g. port range assignments) and, thus, no additional implementation costs will arise. In contrast, the split and merge at software will increase the computational costs because bit shifts and bit concatenate operations will be necessary.

Dedicated Another method would be to transmit a dedicated FSL data word for each port. Hence, it would limit the maximum bit-width of each ports' event value data type to 31 bit which may be impractical for certain use cases. Another downside of this approach is the high number of data words which have to be transmitted over FSL if only ports with small bit-widths are used. However, no additional cost would incur at the software or hardware part related to split and merge of the ports event values.

Address SynDEVS Ports will possibly not emit an event value at every discrete point in time. Thus, only the needed port events could be transmitted over FSL. Each event has to be marked with an identifier to which port it relates. Such a port addressing would cost $a = \lceil \log_2(n) \rceil$ bits. If the port address will be transmitted with the event value within a single data

Table 4.2 Comparison of the different SynDEVS port mapping methods to the 32-bit bounded FSL communication interface

Type	Upper bound for ports or port bit-widths	Required FSL data words	Fixed time[a]	Software overhead[b]
Parallel	$n + \sum_{i=1}^{n} |p_i| = m \leq 32$	1	✓	✓
Split	none	$\left\lceil \frac{m}{32} \right\rceil$	✓	✓
Dedicated[c]	$|p_i| \leq 31$	$|p_i|$	✓	✓
	(none)	$(\sum_{i=1}^{n} \left\lceil \frac{|p_i|+1}{32} \right\rceil)$	(✓)	(✓)
Address[c]	$|p_i| \leq 32$	$\leq |p_i|$	–	–
	(none)	$(\leq \sum_{i=1}^{n} \left\lceil \frac{|p_i|}{32} \right\rceil)$	(–)	(✓)

[a] Marked if the communication time of a SynDEVS model may be evaluated statically (i.e. without consideration of event occurrence).

[b] Marked if the software implementation of the SynDEVS model needs complex operations (i.e. shift or bit concatenation operations) for encoding the events within the FSL data word.

[c] Both mapping types, *Dedicated* and *Address*, may split the event value across multiple FSL data words for the cost of additional computational overhead.

word, the maximum bit-width of event values would further decrease to $32 - a$ bits. Such an encoding would increase the computational cost at the software implementation again. Another approach would be to transmit the address as an own data word followed by a second data word with the event value. Thus, the communication costs would double but no additional computation costs at the software implementation would arise.

Table 4.2 depicts a comparison of the different port mappings. For each mapping it is summarized, if an upper bound for the amount of ports or the ports bit-widths exists. Additionally, the amount of FSL data words required to transmit the event values is given. Ratings are included if the communication time is fixed and if the mapping involves further complex computation operations on the software part of the SynDEVS model.

The *Split* type was chosen as the port mapping implemented in the automatic FSL interface generation because the balance between communication time and computational overhead for encoding events is superior. The *Dedicated* solution features almost no software overhead but is very inefficient for transmitting a lot of low bit-width events. In contrast, the *Address* type is most efficient regarding the communication costs but additional software overhead will be introduced for iterating over each active port and, thus, selectively transmit event values.

FSL Interface Generation

During the communication interface generation, the toplevel parallel component of the SynDEVS model hardware part will be enriched with two FSL-related communication components. Thus, both, a FSL receiver and a FSL transmitter component, will be generated.

The transmitter component will react on any input event it receives from the wrapped toplevel hardware component and transmit the events over FSL to the software part. Therefore, the different input events received over each input port have to be mapped with the *Split* mapping to appropriate FSL data words. For this purpose, the FSL transmitter will make a snapshot of its input ports and serialize the events over multiple FSL data words. New received events during the serialization will be ignored and, thus, the model has to be checked against its event transmit rate. For simplification of the transmit process, no handshake protocol was implemented. However, this does not limit the approach because components with a high event rate will be more likely placed in hardware than in software. Please note that SynDEVS models implemented as software executed on a MicroBlaze

Figure 4.13 GUI screenshot of two atomic com-
ponents bound to hard-
ware and software in-
stances.

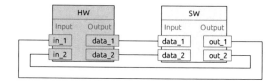

processor are about two orders of magnitude slower than implemented in
hardware.

The receiver part is split into two different components. The first component will receive the 32-bit FSL data word and the second component will
de-serialize the data words into events. Thus, regardless of the amount of
received FSL data words, all events will occur at once within the SynDEVS
models hardware part after the de-serialization.

Figure 4.13 depict two atomic components connected to each other over
two input and two output ports. The *HW* component (i.e. blue) is bound
to a hardware instance and the *SW* component (i.e. yellow) to a software
instance. Thus, the events which occur on the output ports $P_{out,data\_1}$ and
$P_{out,data\_2}$ of the HW component have to be transmitted over FSL to the
software part. Similarly, all events from the output ports P_{out,out_1} and
P_{out,out_2} of the SW component have to be transmitted over FSL back to the
hardware part input ports P_{in,in_1} and P_{in,in_2}.

Figure 4.14 depicts the resulting SynDEVS model hardware part after
automated FSL interface generation. Events incoming from the software
part over the FSL are received by the *FSL* component. Specifically, this component only receives the FSL data words which will be afterwards relayed
to the *FSL_2_SynDEVS* component. Then, the events are de-serialized from
the data words by exploiting the *Split* mapping and send to the wrapped
original hardware part. Similarly, all emitted events are transmitted to the
software part by exploiting the *SynDEVS_2_FSL* component. The scheduling of the events (i.e. which input port event value bit will be placed in
which bit of the *i*-th FSL data word) will be automatically done during
the transformation process and, thus, is fixed for the *Split* mapping type.
Hence, exploiting a fixed splitting the required computation for serialization and de-serialization at the hardware part is minimal.

In contrast, at the SynDEVS models software part no additional atomic
components for receiving or transmitting events will be introduced because FSL communication capability is an intrinsic property of the exploited

Figure 4.14 GUI screen-shot of the three auto-matically generated FSL communication inter-face components for the hardware part of the Syn-DEVS model. The two input and output ports of the *Toplevel_HW* are connected over FSL to the SynDEVS models soft-ware parts.

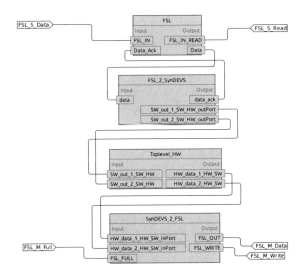

MicroBlaze architecture. Thus, only a software communication driver will be generated in terms of C++ source code which implements the required binding for the *Split* mapping. However, bit shift operations and bit con-catenations are required during the mapping. Both operation types may be executed on a MicroBlaze processor by exploiting a single clock cycle instruction and, thus, the mapping is highly efficient regarding the compu-tational overhead, too.

Listing 4.9 depicts the generated source code for the software part. The FSL will be queried non-blocking to retrieve any new events from the hard-ware part at each software model evaluation cycle. Afterwards, the events are de-serialized in the port_event_handler() function and relayed to the SynDEVS model software part in the updateDevsInports() func-tion. Transmission of events from the software part to the hardware part is handled by the sendEvents() function. Thus, each output port is queried for an active event and serialized to the FSL data word.

Listing 4.9 Automatically generated source code of the FSL communication inter-face for the SynDEVS model software part

```
1 #include "portdriver_fsl.h"
2
3 PortDriver_FSL :: PortDriver_FSL () {
4    // set inputs to invalid
5    inEvents.HW_data_1_HW_SW_enable = false;
```

```
 6    inEvents.HW_data_2_HW_SW_enable = false ;
 7  }
 8
 9  void PortDriver_FSL :: port_event_handler () {
10    register uint32_t fsl_in ;
11    // Copy/Retrieve Events/Data
12    getfsl (fsl_in , 0);
13    inEvents.HW_data_1_HW_SW = (( fsl_in >> 2) & 0x1); // Get bits 2:2
14    inEvents.HW_data_1_HW_SW_enable = (( fsl_in >> 0) & 0x1); // Enable
          retrieved from bit 0
15    inEvents.HW_data_2_HW_SW = (( fsl_in >> 3) & 0x1); // Get bits 3:3
16    inEvents.HW_data_2_HW_SW_enable = (( fsl_in >> 1) & 0x1); // Enable
          retrieved from bit 1
17  }
18
19  void PortDriver_FSL :: sendEvents () {
20    register uint32_t fsl_out = 0;
21    // Copy/Set Events/Data
22    if (DevsModel :: hasEventAtOutport_sw_out_1_sw_hw ()) {
23      fsl_out |= (( DevsModel :: getDataFromOutport_sw_out_1_sw_hw ()) & 0
            x1) << 2; // Set bits 2:2
24      fsl_out |= 0x1; // Enable stored at bit 0
25    }
26    if (DevsModel :: hasEventAtOutport_sw_out_2_sw_hw ()) {
27      fsl_out |= (( DevsModel :: getDataFromOutport_sw_out_2_sw_hw ()) & 0
            x1) << 3; // Set bits 3:3
28      fsl_out |= 0x2; // Enable stored at bit 1
29    }
30    // Send all ports and their enable signals
31    putfsl (fsl_out ,0) ;
32  }
33
34  void PortDriver_FSL :: updateDevsInports () {
35    if (inEvents.HW_data_1_HW_SW_enable) {
36      DevsModel :: setDataForInport_hw_data_1_hw_sw (inEvents.
            HW_data_1_HW_SW) ;
37      inEvents.HW_data_1_HW_SW_enable = false ;
38    }
39    if (inEvents.HW_data_2_HW_SW_enable) {
40      DevsModel :: setDataForInport_hw_data_2_hw_sw (inEvents.
            HW_data_2_HW_SW) ;
41      inEvents.HW_data_2_HW_SW_enable = false ;
42    }
43  }
```

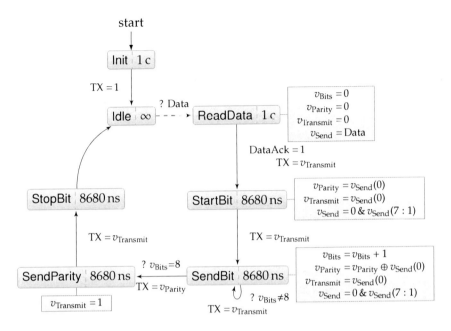

Figure 4.15 UART transmitter modelled as an atomic component

Application Example

An UART transmitter component was implemented as a proof-of-concept for the SynDEVS model to C++ source code transformation process. Thus, the application example of the SynDEVS to VHDL source code transformation process was considered, cf. Section 4.2.2, but only the transmitter component was implemented in software. The rest of the SynDEVS model was implement in hardware and an automatically generated FSL interface in between both SynDEVS model parts was exploited.

Figure 4.15 depicts the atomic component of the UART transmitter implemented in software. It allows transmission of UART data with 115,000 baud, 8 data bits, 1 start bit, 1 stop bit and an even parity bit. Please note that the smallest timeout value $\tau(s)$ is $8.68\mu s$. Thus, the MicroBlaze has to be able to execute each evaluation cycle of the SynDEVS model within this strict timing constraint.

For the implemented MicroBlaze, running the software part of the SynDEVS model with a clock rate of 100 MHz, a profiling was done. Both, the MicroBlaze soft-core processor and the VHDL IP core implementing the rest of the SynDEVS model's UART transceiver, were simulated with a VHDL simulator (i.e. Mentor Graphics ModelSim 6.6d). The MicroBlaze PC[18] register was watched and, thus, the time needed for executing the ISR[19] (i.e. running a single evaluation cycle of the SynDEVS model) was profiled. The execution time of the ISR depends upon the state of the transmitter component to be executed. Some states have annotated more complex computations. However, approx. $5.9\mu s$ are needed to execute a single evaluation cycle and, thus, the SynDEVS model is able to be executed on the MicroBlaze processor in real-time. Hence, it was implemented on a Virtex-5 FPGA and successfully executed (i.e. a PC connected over the serial line to the FPGA board received the transmitted data successfully). Section A.4 includes the complete listing of the UART transmitter component transformed from SynDEVS to C++ source code. However, this basic application example is not detailed further (e.g. resource consumption), because a far more complex application example including legacy source code integration will be featured in Section 6.2.

---

[18] *Program Counter*

[19] *Interrupt Service Routine*

CHAPTER 5

Graphical User Interface

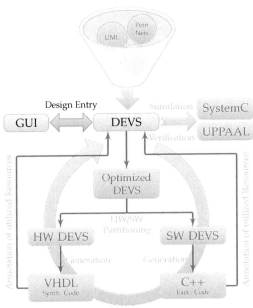

In this chapter, a graphical user interface for the SynDEVS MoC will be presented. The GUI and all command line tools implementing the steps of the presented hardware / software co-design flow have been written in C++ source code. The *Qt* cross-platform application and UI framework [Nok11] was exploited to allow tool usage on a broad range of operating systems (i.e. Microsoft Windows, Mac OS, and Linux).

The GUI allows the creation and editing of SynDEVS models. The designer of a SynDEVS model must not specify the model directly as SCXML source code which is a tedious and error-prone task, instead the model may be specified by using the GUI exploiting the visual programming paradigm. Furthermore, all intermediate models of the presented design flow may be reviewed within the GUI. For instance, after partitioning a model in software and hardware instances, a FSL communication interface will be generated and, thus, the modified model of the hardware instance including the introduced atomic components for the communication interface may be analysed within the GUI.

An in depth discussion of all exploited methods and concepts of the GUI and its tools, implemented within approx. 24,000 lines of source code, would go far beyond the scope of this thesis. Instead, only a short overview of the GUI will be given in the rest of this chapter for brevity. Furthermore, specification and parsing of variable and output port assignments and transition conditions will be discussed for both, the GUI and the SCXML file format of SynDEVS models. Afterwards, the generation of C++ and VHDL source code for these parsed arithmetic and logical expressions will be detailed by some illustrative examples.

5.1 SynDEVS Model Editor

Figure 5.1 depicts the main interface of the GUI for the SynDEVS MoC. The inner main view of the GUI displays the SynDEVS models. This view will show either the contents of a parallel component or the contents of an atomic component. In Figure 5.1, the inner atomic components (e.g. *ArithCtrl*) of a parallel component are depicted together with the parallel components input and output ports (e.g. *src*). New ports, components, or connections may be visually added by using the top tool bars' buttons. All editing operations will be registered at the *Undo Stack*, which is placed on the right side of the GUI. Thus, every single editing operation may be undone by

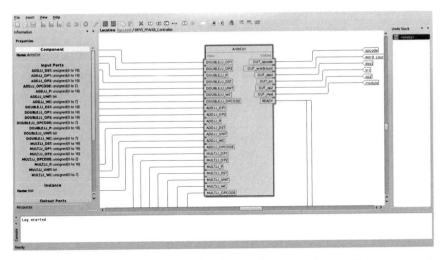

Figure 5.1 Screenshot for the hierarchical view (i.e. view of a parallel component) of the Graphical User Interface

the designer. Such a basic feature is of utmost importance for modelling convenience, hence, some embedded platform development tools (e.g. Xilinx EDK) do not provide an undone feature, which may result in tedious work after the model was erroneously changed.

The *Information* panel on the left side of the GUI depicts additional information for the currently selected element. For instance, all input ports names and their types are listed if the *ArithCtrl* atomic component is selected. The user interface will enforce a lot of modelling rules and, thus, will minimize modelling errors. For example, it is not possible to connect input and output ports with different types.

All steps of the hardware / software co-design flow may be centrally executed from the GUI. Thus, log messages (e.g. errors) will be displayed in the *Console* log at the bottom of the GUI. However, each step of the design flow may be additionally executed by its own executable program. Thus, it is easy to embed the design flow steps into customized work flows (e.g. a *Makefile* script).

Figure 5.2 depicts a screenshot of the GUI showing the state view of an atomic component. Basically, the graphical representation introduced in Section 2.4 is exploited but modified slightly for better representation on screen (e.g. no background colour for states or the initial state is shown with

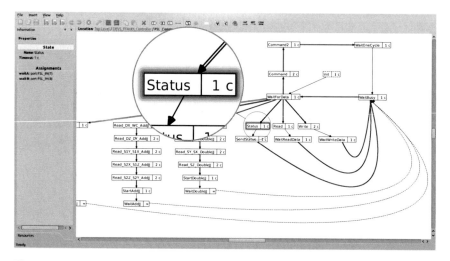

Figure 5.2 Screenshot for the state view (i.e. view of an atomic component) of the Graphical User Interface

a dashed border). However, all key elements are identically represented. For instance, an internal transition is depicted by a simple arrow line but a confluent transition is shown with a double arrow line. In contrast, the variable assignments or transition conditions are hidden and, thus, may be viewed by hovering with the mouse cursor over tan element (i.e. additional information is shown at the left panel). Conditions or assignments may be edited by opening an edit dialog (i.e. double clicking the element). A lot of syntax checks will be performed at the entered conditions or variable and output port assignments. For instance, it is checked if an used port name within an arithmetic expression is known at the atomic component or if an input port is erroneous exploited at an internal transition.

5.2 SynDEVS MoC SCXML File Format Handling

The SynDEVS models created with the GUI will be saved in SCXML file format as detailed in [MSH09]. However, some additional tags and types were introduced to specify the visual layout of components, states, ports, and so on within the GUI. Internally, all exploited SynDEVS elements are represented by their own specific class storing all necessary informations (e.g. component name or connection source and sink). Figure 5.3

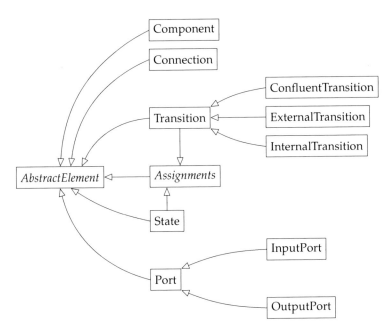

Figure 5.3 Class hierarchy for SynDEVS model representation

depict the hierarchy of the most important classes for SynDEVS representation. These classes' objects represent both the structure and the behaviour of a SynDEVS model. However, by exploiting the GUI, each object (e.g. Component) is linked with another specific class implementing the visual representation and behaviour of that object within the GUI (e.g. ComponentGUI). By doing so, the models visual appearance and GUI-specific behaviour is strictly separated from the SynDEVS-specific model behaviour and structure. This is very beneficial for the development of the miscellaneous hardware / software co-design tools (e.g. optimization of zero-timeout states). Then, these non-graphical tools may exploit the same classes for representing the SynDEVS model without reinventing the wheel for handling the structure and behaviour of SynDEVS models. Thus, each SynDEVS SCXML file may be automatically parsed into objects representing the whole SynDEVS model. In addition, the tools may modify the model by calling a set of diverse objects functions and, afterwards, the objects may be automatically stored back into SCXML file format. By exploiting a substantial subset of the GUI's source code, development of new tools is very efficient and safe because most of the SynDEVS MoC rules (e.g. only a single output port may be connected to an input port of an atomic component) are checked during runtime by the exploited classes.

Most class representations of the various SynDEVS model aspects are simple and may be implemented straightforward. However, a lot of effort has to be put into parsing the expressions of the transition conditions and variable and output port assignments, which will be detailed in the latter.

5.3 Arithmetic and Logical Expressions

Expressions may be used at transition conditions as well as output port and variable assignments. Depending upon the use case, one of three different types of expressions have to be parsed. For instance, if an expression is exploited at the assignment of variables or output ports only arithmetic expressions are allowed. However, if an expression is used to define a transition condition additional logical expressions and conditions may be exploited. Even more, only variable values may be accessed within an internal transition condition. In contrast, an external or confluent transition may exploit both, input ports and variables, within the expression of the transition condition. In the following, these different expressions are defined in BNF[1] [Knu64] and discussed in detail.

Binary, decimal, and hexadecimal values as well as bit vectors are defined by:

⟨Digit⟩ → 0 | 1 | 2 | 3 | 4 | 5 | 6 | 7 | 8 | 9
⟨Integer⟩ → ⟨Digit⟩ | ⟨Digit⟩ ⟨Integer⟩
⟨BinDigit⟩ → 0 | 1
⟨Bin⟩ → ⟨BinDigit⟩ | ⟨BinDigit⟩ ⟨Bin⟩
⟨HexDigit⟩ → ⟨Digit⟩ | A | B | C | ... | F | a | b | c | ... | f
⟨Hex⟩ → ⟨HexDigit⟩ | ⟨HexDigit⟩ ⟨Hex⟩
⟨Hex-BitVector⟩ → x" ⟨Hex⟩ "
⟨Bin-BitVector⟩ → " ⟨Bin⟩ "
⟨BitVector⟩ → ⟨Hex-BitVector⟩ | ⟨Bin-BitVector⟩

Variable, port, and component names may only contain basic characters, numbers, or underscores. A name may not start with a numbers to avoid

---

[1] *Backus-Naur Form*

ambiguity against parsing a decimal value. Thus, instance names are defined by the following BNF rules:

⟨Char⟩ → A | B | C | ... | Z | a | b | c | ... | z
⟨CharDigit_⟩ → ⟨Char⟩ | ⟨Digit⟩ | _
⟨Name-Pre⟩ → ⟨Char⟩ | _
⟨Name-Post⟩ → ⟨CharDigit_⟩ | ⟨CharDigit_⟩ ⟨Name-Post⟩
⟨Name⟩ → ⟨Name-Pre⟩ ⟨Name-Post⟩

Parsing of global constants, ports, and variables differs between the GUI and SCXML. Within SCXML, a reference to these instances has to be done by a XPath expression which is very long and tedious to write (e.g. **inst-ance**(`'Component'`)/**port**[**name**=`'input'`]). Thus, a shorter notation (e.g. **port**:`input`) was introduced within the GUI for accessing these instances. For the SCXML file format, these instances are parsed by the following BNF rules:

⟨Constant-Name⟩ →
    instance(`'General_information'`)/
    constant[**name**=`'` ⟨Name⟩ `'`]
⟨Port⟩ →
    instance(`'` ⟨Name⟩ `_data'`)/
    port[**name**=`'` ⟨Name⟩ `'`]
⟨Variable⟩ →
    instance(`'` ⟨Name⟩ `_data'`)/
    variable[**name**=`'` ⟨Name⟩]

In contrast, the following rules define the shorter version which will be exploiting within the GUI:

⟨Constant-Name⟩ → / ⟨Name⟩ /
⟨Port⟩ → **port**: ⟨Name⟩
⟨Variable⟩ → **variable**: ⟨Name⟩

However, a constant may be either a decimal value, a bit vector, or a reference to a global constant:

⟨Constant⟩ → ⟨Integer⟩ | ⟨BitVector⟩ | ⟨Constant-Name⟩

Whenever ports or variables are exploited, it is possible to specify a specific bit or a bit range after the port or variable reference:

⟨Port-Range⟩ →
　　　⟨Port⟩ |
　　　⟨Port⟩ (⟨Integer⟩) |
　　　⟨Port⟩ (⟨Integer⟩ : ⟨Integer⟩)
⟨Variable-Range⟩ →
　　　⟨Variable⟩ |
　　　⟨Variable⟩ (⟨Integer⟩) |
　　　⟨Variable⟩ (⟨Integer⟩ : ⟨Integer⟩)

As a proof-of-concept, arithmetic expressions may exploit the following operations: Modulo (%), concatenation (&), negation (`not` or -), addition (+), subtraction (-), and multiplication (*). Without further ado, it is possible to extend the grammar to support more operations. Thus, arithmetic expressions, which take into account the evaluation order of multiplications against additions, are defined by:

⟨Function⟩ → **unsigned** | **signed**
⟨MulExpr⟩ →
　　　⟨UnaryExpr⟩ |
　　　⟨MulExpr⟩ * ⟨UnaryExpr⟩
⟨AtomExpr⟩ →
　　　⟨Constant⟩ |
　　　⟨Variable-Range⟩ |
　　　⟨Port-Range⟩ |
　　　(⟨Expr⟩) |
　　　⟨Function⟩ (⟨Expr⟩)
⟨UnaryExpr⟩ →
　　　⟨AtomExpr⟩ |
　　　- ⟨AtomExpr⟩ |
　　　not ⟨AtomExpr⟩
⟨AddExpr-Op⟩ → % | + | - | &
⟨AddExpr⟩ →
　　　⟨MulExpr⟩ |
　　　⟨AddExpr⟩ ⟨AddExpr-Op⟩ ⟨MulExpr⟩
⟨Expr⟩ → ⟨AddExpr⟩

Logic expression are parsed by the following rules:

⟨Equation-Op⟩ → = | != | <= | >= | < | >
⟨Equation⟩ → ⟨Variable-Range⟩ ⟨Equation-Op⟩ ⟨Expr⟩
⟨AtomExpr⟩ → ⟨Equation⟩ | (⟨LogExpr⟩)
⟨UnaryLogExpr⟩ →
      ⟨AtomExpr⟩ |
      not ⟨AtomLogExpr⟩
⟨AndLogExpr-Op⟩ → **and** | **or** | **xor**
⟨AndLogExpr⟩ →
      ⟨UnaryLogExpr⟩ |
      ⟨AndLogExpr⟩ ⟨AndLogExpr-Op⟩ ⟨UnaryLogExpr⟩
⟨LogExpr⟩ → ⟨AndLogExpr⟩

Taken all previously defined rules into account, an internal transition condition may be parsed by starting from the ⟨LogExpr⟩ rule. In addition, parsing the conditions of external or confluent transitions, the previously defined rules have to be further extended:

⟨Active⟩ → **active**
⟨Equation⟩ →
      ⟨Port-Range⟩ = ⟨Active⟩ |
      ⟨Port-Range⟩ ⟨Equation-Op⟩ ⟨Expr⟩ |
      ⟨Variable-Range⟩ ⟨Equation-Op⟩ ⟨Expr⟩

Port and variable assignments may feature conditional and sequential assignments. Thus, the previous rules have to be further extended by the following BNF rules:

⟨AddExpr-Op⟩ → % | + | - | **and** | **or** | **xor** | &
⟨Case⟩ → ⟨LogExpr⟩ : ⟨Sequence⟩
⟨Case-Sequence⟩ → ⟨Case⟩ | ⟨Case-Sequence⟩ , ⟨Case⟩
⟨Expr⟩ →
      # | *(no operation)*
      (⟨LogExpr⟩ ? ⟨Sequence⟩ : ⟨Sequence⟩) |
      { ⟨Case-Sequence⟩ } |
      { ⟨Case-Sequence⟩ , ⟨Sequence⟩ } |
      ⟨AddExpr⟩
⟨Sequence⟩ → ⟨Expr⟩ | ⟨Sequence⟩ ; ⟨Expr⟩

In contrast to the parsing of a transition condition, which starts parsing at the ⟨LogExpr⟩ rule, the right side of a variable or output port assignment may be parsed by starting at the ⟨Sequence⟩ rule.

5.4 Expression Parser Implementation

The BNF rules of Section 5.3 are implemented by exploiting Flex [VM07] and Bison [Fre11]. Flex is a tool for generation a lexical scanner. Thus, it recognises lexical patterns in text files or strings and return tokens (e.g. a port name or a decimal value). These tokens will be used by Bison which is a parser generator. Bison generates C or C++ source code for a grammar of the language to be parsed. The language grammar given to the Bison parser generator has to be a deterministic context-free grammar, which may be efficiently parsed by a LR(1) parsing algorithm [AJ74]. By doing so, the before mentioned expressions may be parsed into an AST wherein each tree node represents an arithmetic or logical expression and each tree leaf represents a value (e.g. decimal value or input port). More information about exploiting Flex and Bison to built domain-specific compilers may be found in [Lev09] and, thus, is not detailed here for brevity.

For the SynDEVS model, two different lexical scanners were implemented: Firstly, a scanner for the GUI-specific tokens and, secondly, a scanner for the SCXML-specific XPath tokens, cf. Section 5.3. However, the BNF rules were implemented by a single grammar and, thus, a single Bison language file is exploited. The generated parser may be exploited to parse both, GUI-specific or SCXML-specific expressions, into an intermediate AST representation. The expression objects of the AST (e.g. an object for the addition of values or sub-expressions) may be recursively traversed by the GUI to re-generate the textual representation of the expression in GUI or SCXML file format. Even more, the AST classes may output C++ or VHDL source code. Thus, for each AST element, the textual representation of itself may be given in GUI, SCXML, C++, and VHDL format. Even more, the library generated by the Bison parser generator includes error reporting functionality. Thus, an expression is constantly error-checked while it is entered within the GUI. Whenever an error is detected, the specific location within the condition or assignment expression will be highlighted and reported to the designer. Errors within the specified expressions may be corrected prior to executing the complete hardware / software co-design flow including synthesis of the VHDL source code and compilation of the C++ source code.

5.5 Examples

In the following, some illustrative examples of transition conditions and variable or output port assignments will be given together with the resulting VHDL and C++ code. Please note that the parsing of expressions requires a context (e.g. the component of which the expression is part of or all declared variables within that component). Thus, the following examples will exploit an unsigned 32-bit integer variable named *data* within the atomic component *Transmitter*.

In GUI syntax, a basic increment of a variable is given by the expression

$$\texttt{variable:}\texttt{data+1}$$

which will be parsed into an AST and, afterwards, traversed into the following SCXML, C++, or VHDL expressions:

```
SCXML:  instance('Transmitter_data')/-
        variable[name='data'] + 1
  C++:  (*variable_data) + 1
 VHDL:  data + TO_UNSIGNED(1, 32).
```

A transition condition to check if the input port *RX* is active and if the variable *data* equals eight is

$$\texttt{port:RX=active and variable:}\texttt{data=8}$$

with the following parsing results:

```
SCXML:  instance('Transmitter_data')/port-
        [name='RX']='ACTIVE'and instance('Transmitter_-
        data')/variable[name='data']=8
  C++:  this->inport_RX->isActive && (*variable_data)==8
 VHDL:  RX_enable='1' and data=TO_UNSIGNED(8, 32).
```

An output port assignment from a confluent transition which concatenates the lower seven bits of the variable *data* together with the input port *RX* is

$$\texttt{variable:}\texttt{data(6:0)}\texttt{&port:RX}$$

with the following parsing results:

```
SCXML:  instance('Transmitter_data')/variable-
        [name='data'](6:0) & instance('Transmitter_-
        data')/port[name='RX']
  C++:  (*variable_data>>0 & 127)<<1 | (this->in-
        port_RX->data)
 VHDL:  data(6 downto 0) & RX.
```

Thus, the expression parser's output source code may include additional source code for arithmetic functions which may not be directly exploited within the targeted language. For instance, the given vector range has to be transformed into bit-shift and bit-masking operations for the C++ source code output.

An expression of a variable assignment to the variable *targetName*, including an inner conditional assignment, may be written as

```
(variable:data=x"1337AFFE"?1:variable:data(20:21))
```

with the following parsing results:

SCXML: `{instance('Transmitter_data')/variable[name='data']=x"1337AFFE":1,instance('Transmitter_data')/variable[name='data'](20:21)}`

C++:
```
if ((*variable_data)==0x1337AFFE) {
  targetName = 1;
} else {
  targetName = (*variable_data>>20 & 3);
}
```

VHDL:
```
if data=to_unsigned(16#1337AFFE#,32) then
  targetName <= TO_UNSIGNED(1, 32);
else
  targetName <= data(20 to 21);
end if;.
```

CHAPTER 6

Case Studies

In this chapter, three different case studies will be discussed: First, an application example of a DVI controller will be presented. The developed SynDEVS model has strict real-time requirements and will highlight the *Retiming* step of the presented hardware / software co-design flow.

Second, a more realistic application example of a network-based Pong game will be given. This example features a single SynDEVS model with hardware and software parts. Thus, the whole advocated SynDEVS MoC hardware / software co-design flow will be exploited. Additionally, the reuse of legacy software will be highlighted by embedding a legacy software library (i.e. an Ethernet network stack) into the SynDEVS model.

The last example which will be presented is a more complex application example of a cryptographic accelerator for RSA[1] and ECC[2]. In contrast to both other examples, this case study will demonstrate that an exploitation of the SynDEVS MoC within an existing heterogeneous hardware / software design may be very beneficial. Therefore, a complex SynDEVS model will be implemented in hardware and embedded into the existing system design of a cryptographic accelerator.

6.1 Digital Video Interface Controller

In [MSH11], a SynDEVS model of a DVI [Dig99] controller has been presented to evaluate the hardware-part of the presented hardware / software co-design flow in respect to a model with strict real-time requirements (i.e. DVI signal generation). Specifically, the need of optimizing the zero-timeout states for hardware synthesis will be detailed, cf. Section 4.2.3.

---

[1] *Rivest, Shamir, and Adleman; a public key encryption technology*

[2] *Elliptic Curve Cryptography*

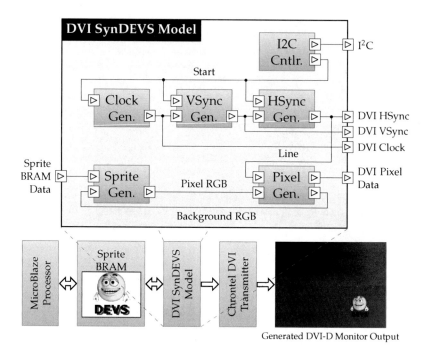

Figure 6.1 Hardware architecture of the Digital Video Interface controller SynDEVS model application example [MSH11]

Figure 6.1 depicts the basic data-flow to generate a DVI monitor signal with a moving sprite on top of a procedural background image and highlights the SynDEVS parallel component of the DVI controller model.

In the lower part of Figure 6.1, the abstract data-flow inside the system is depicted. A MicroBlaze soft-core processor is exploited to initialize a dedicated BRAM with a sprite image. The sprite features transparency and, thus, four bytes (i.e. red, green, blue, and alpha values) are stored for each sprite pixel. The sprite's pixels are read by the DVI SynDEVS model to intermix them with a procedurally generated background image. Thus, opaque pixels of the sprite will replace the background pixels and transparent pixels will be alpha-blended [PD84] with the opaque background pixels. Afterwards, the evaluated pixel value will be send to the DVI transmitter chip (i.e. a Chrontel CH7301C [Chr10]) of the exploited FPGA board

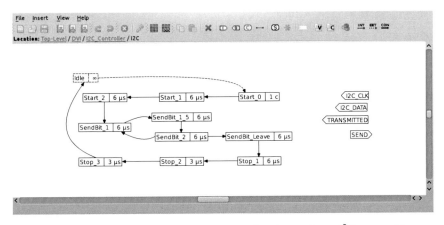

Figure 6.2 Screenshot of an atomic component implementing a I^2C transmitter

to display it on a connected TFT[3] monitor. The outputted screen picture is shown on the right of Figure 6.1. Please note that the position of the sprite will be changed each DVI frame and, thus, it is constantly moving around and will bounce at the screen borders. In contrast to a regular graphic card with dedicated display memory for DVI output of a pre-calculated screen image, the SynDEVS model of the DVI transmitter calculates each pixel's value during runtime and, thus, features a strict real-time requirement.

In the upper part of Figure 6.1, the SynDEVS model is depicted in detail. The exploited Chrontel DVI transmitter chip has to be initialized prior the output of DVI data. Therefore, a I^2C[4] transceiver (i.e. *I2C Cntlr.*) is included to send the required power-up command sequence over I^2C. After the DVI transmitter was successfully initialized, a start event will be issued to all other components of the SynDEVS model to generate the DVI signals. The *Clock Gen.*, *VSync Gen.*, and *HSync Gen.* components will generate the DVI timing signals for controlling the cathode ray of the monitor which will define the position of the transmitted DVI pixel on screen. The *DVI Clock* signal is the fastest one of the generated clock signals and has a period of 40 ns regarding the chosen output resolution of 640 × 480 at 60 Hz. Thus, the background pixel values have to be evaluated and intermixed with the translucent sprite pixel within this period. Furthermore, the sprite will cover only a small portion of the screen and, thus, the current pixel position

---

[3] *Thin-Film Transistor*

[4] *Inter-Integrated Circuit; generically referred to as* two-wire interface

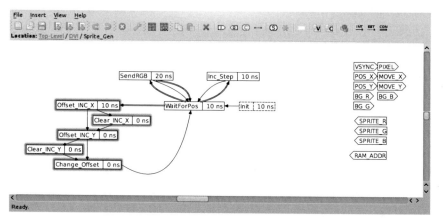

Figure 6.3 Screenshot of a zero-timeout state chain which has to be optimized during the hardware / software co-design flow

has to be checked against the sprite's boundary.

6.1.1 Time Flow

The embedded I^2C transmitter atomic component depicted by Figure 6.2 implements the I^2C Standard-mode protocol [NXP12] (i.e. transmission speeds up to 100 kBit/s). The basic implementation method of the I^2C transmitter is similar to the UART transmitter, cf. Section 4.2.2, and, thus, is not detailed for brevity. However, the time flow of the I^2C protocol may be directly expressed by state timeout annotations within the SynDEVS model, cf. Figure 6.2, which is very beneficial compared to a hardware description language (e.g. VHDL), cf. Section 4.2.2. The designer of the model may extract the required I^2C timing directly from the specification and natively express it as state timeout annotations. Thus, once gained domain-specific knowledge is not lost and may be mapped directly into the SynDEVS model.

6.1.2 Control Flow

In Figure 6.3, the *Sprite Gen.* atomic component is highlighted. The component will retrieve the sprite's pixel value for a given screen coordinate. Therefore, it has to be checked if the given coordinate is within the boundary of the sprite and, then, the sprite pixel is loaded from the BRAM and alpha-blended to the retrieved background pixel. Afterwards, the new pixel value will be transmitted back to the requesting component (i.e. *Pixel Gen.*). If the current screen coordinate is outside of the sprite's boundary then the unmodified background pixel will be transmitted back. Additionally, the sprite may be moved after each frame into, both, vertical and horizontal direction on the screen. Therefore, the highlighted zero-timeout state chain will update the sprite's x and y coordinate conditionally according to the requested move directions. At the Offset_INC_X state, the horizontal sprite position will be updated if a horizontal move is requested. Afterwards, the internal transition to the Clear$_I$NC$_X$ state will be taken if the sprite has either hit the left or right border of the screen. Within this state, the vector of the horizontal move direction will be mirrored (i.e. the sprite bounces off at the screen borders). Then, the vertical sprite position will be updated and corrected in case of need. Afterwards, the sprite's position will be set to the evaluated changed position.

Modelling these conditional computations, both, in space and time is very beneficial: Firstly, the model state space directly represent the activities of the model (e.g. move sprite in horizontal direction) and secondly, the zero-timeout chain ensures that the model's activity last only a specific duration (i.e. the new sprite position will be determined within 10 ns). Clearly, the highlighted chain of zero-timeout states could be reduced to a single state with 10 ns timeout in terms of executing the state optimization algorithm by hand, cf. Section 4.2.3, but with a reduced readability of the model. Therefore, zero-timeout states are a fundamental concept within SynDEVS MoC to model control flow with strict timing-requirements, if the visual expressiveness of the model is of utmost interest.

6.1.3 Results

The DVI controller application example was synthesized for the Xilinx Virtex-5 FPGA of the XUPv5-LX110T Development System. In [MSH11], two different versions were implemented: Firstly, an unoptimized version of the SynDEVS model which features zero-timeout state chains for conditional execution of model parts and secondly, an optimized version in which the zero-timeout state chains were aggregated into adjacent non-zero timeout states, cf. Section 4.2.3. Thus, both version exploit the same SynDEVS input model but for the unoptimized version the *Retiming* step of the hardware / software co-design flow was omitted, cf. Figure 4.1.

Table 6.1 Synthesis results of the Digital Video Interface controller SynDEVS model [MSH11]

	SynDEVS		Slice Logic Utilization		Clock Frequency
	States	Trans.	Registers	LUTs	
Unoptimized	66	77	376	692	500 MHz
Optimized	61	73	370	614	100 MHz
Improvement	8.2 %	5.5 %	1.6 %	12.7 %	400 %

Table 6.1 depicts the figures of merit for both versions. The unoptimized version of the SynDEVS model features a timing requirement of 500 MHz due to the zero-timeout state chain of the *Sprite Gen.* component, cf. Figure 6.3. The zero-timeout state chain is of length $n = 4$ and, thus, the timing requirement of the SynDEVS model will be after synthesis

$$\tau_{gcd} = \frac{10\,ns}{4 + 1} = 2\,ns = 500\,MHz$$

according to the calculation detailed in Section 4.2.2. However, it is needless to point out that on the exploited Xilinx Virtex-5 FPGA such a high timing requirement cannot be easily achieved which results in an unimplementable DVI controller. Therefore, the optimized version of the SynDEVS model additionally exploits the *Retiming* step of the hardware / software co-design flow which results in an implementable controller with a clock period of 10 ns. Hence, the optimization of the SynDEVS model is not only beneficial for the timing requirement but for resource utilization as well. The intermediate SynDEVS model (i.e. the optimized SynDEVS model without zero-timeout state chains) which is transformed into synthesizable VHDL features less states and transitions. Thus, the synthesis output of the optimized version utilizes less registers and LUTs in comparison to the unoptimized version. For instance, the LUT utilization is decreased by more than 10 %.

6.2 Network-based Pong Game

A realistic application example, a network-based *Pong* game with DVI output was implemented to demonstrate, both, the feasibility and the benefits

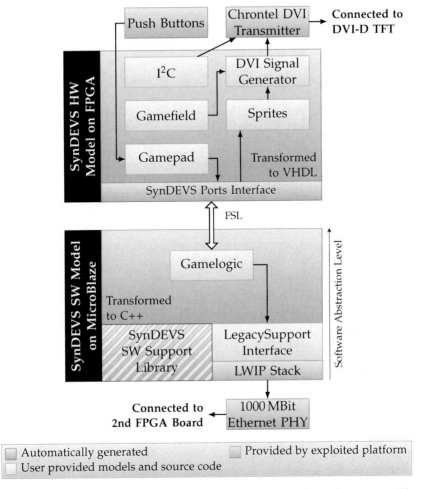

Figure 6.4 Hardware / software architecture of the network-based Pong game. The SynDEVS model exploits a Xilinx MicroBlaze soft-core processor to run the game logic and the network stack integrated as a legacy software library.

of the different hardware / software co-design flow aspects. The SynDEVS model of the Pong game features the integration of legacy C / C++ source code as well as strict real-time requirements. The well-known classic Pong game was one of the first two player games, where both players are controlling a racket up and down while a ball is moving over the game field,

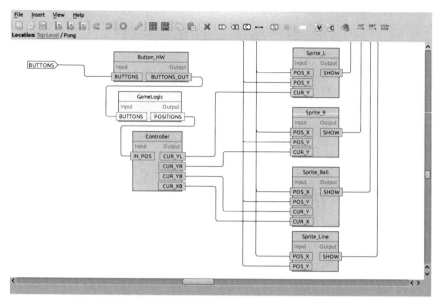

Figure 6.5 Screenshot depicting a part of the SynDEVS model for the network-based Pong game. Components marked blue will be implemented in hardware while yellow marked components are targeted for software implementation.

which must be hit to impede that the adversary scores a point. However, the implemented SynDEVS version of the Pong game involves hard real-time requirements to draw the game field, rackets, and the ball over DVI and reactive parts for implementing both, the game logic and the network communication, to allow a smooth gaming experience. Thus, it is very beneficial to exploit a timed MoC (e.g. SynDEVS MoC) to specify the system behaviour.

6.2.1 SynDEVS Model

Figure 6.4 depicts the resulting hardware / software architecture of the SynDEVS model, which was completely implemented on the Xilinx Virtex-5 FPGA of the XUPv5-LX110T development system. To play the game, two XUPv5 development boards have to be connected over Ethernet network. One of the boards has to be configured to be the game master, which implements the game logic, whereas the second board will solely act as

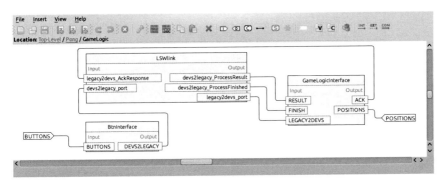

Figure 6.6 Screenshot of the dedicated *LSWlink* atomic component for legacy source code integration

a game client. Please note that the behaviour of both, the game master and the game client, is implement by a single SynDEVS model only. Both boards will display the game field over DVI to each player but the game client board will only receive game field updates from the game master and transmit the user input of the second player back to the master. Thus, the master board handles the complete game logic. However, the DVI controller from Section 6.1 was taken as a foundation in order to implement the DVI game field output.

On the top part of Figure 6.4, the hardware implementation is outlined, which generates the DVI output and recognizes user input. The user may press the development board's push buttons to move one of the rackets. Thus, the *Gamepad* component recognizes the button presses and generates events to be further processed by the software part running the game logic and the network stack.

On the bottom part, the software architecture of the SynDEVS model is illustrated. The topmost layer is the most abstract one, executing the software part of the SynDEVS model. The *Gamelogic* component handles the complete Pong game logic (i.e. racket and ball movements) in software. Thus, it is targeted for software implementation within the SynDEVS model, cf. Figure 6.5. This component exploits the XUPv5 development board's Ethernet network functionality with the help of a light-weight network stack (i.e. *LWIP Stack* [Xil12, pp. 147-160]). The network stack was integrated as a legacy source code library by exploiting the dedicated *LSWlink* atomic component described in Section 4.3.1. Thus, this dedicated atomic component is included within the *Gamelogic* component, cf. Figure 6.6.

Table 6.2 Synthesis and compilation results after the SynDEVS model transformations to embeddable C++ source code and synthesizable VHDL source code

Part	SynDEVS Model Statistics Components	States	Transitions
Software	4	11	14
Hardware	13	69	74

Part	Transformation to C++ Source Code Code Size	Data Size
SynDEVS Model	220 bytes	112 bytes
Support Library	3,264 bytes	40 bytes
Legacy Interface	4,523 bytes	104 bytes

Part	Transformation to VHDL Source Code LUTs	Registers
SynDEVS Model	721	482
Port Interface	48	47

6.2.2 Results

Table 6.2 depicts the results after executing the hardware / software co-design flow for the network-based Pong game. First, the number of exploited components, states, and transitions of the SynDEVS model parts for both instances (i.e. hardware and software) are given.

Second, the transformation results for the software instance are listed. For each part of the software instance, the code and data sizes are given. The *SynDEVS Model* part depicts the required code and data memory sizes for the transformed SynDEVS model (i.e. the behaviour of the model) which scales linearly with the number of exploited components, states, and transitions. In contrast, the *Support Library* part lists the memory requirements for executing the SynDEVS MoC which is constant but will vary for each exploited target architecture (e.g. Xilinx MicroBlaze soft-core processor). However, the *Legacy Interface* part depicts the code and data sizes for implementing the *LWIP Stack* as a legacy source code library and, thus, it memory requirements depends solely on the exploited legacy source code library.

Thirdly, the transformation results for the hardware instance are listed. The results are divided into the *SynDEVS Model* part (i.e. the behaviour of the model) and the *Port Interface* part (i.e. the automatically generated FSL communication interface). In comparison with the synthesis results of the pure DVI controller from Section 6.1.3, the resource consumption has slightly increased because of implementing more sprites (i.e. a sprite for the ball, the game field, and the two rackets). These figures results directly from a Xilinx synthesis run the optimized SynDEVS model after automated FSL communication interface generation (i.e. for the pure *SynDEVS HW Model* part of Figure 4.1).

Both, the exploited MicroBlaze soft-core processor and the generated VHDL source code are clocked with 100 MHz. Then, the game field updates and the push button states are synchronized over the Ethernet link between the game master and game client FPGA boards every 5 ms, which allows a real-time gaming experience.

6.3 Cryptographic Accelerator

In the following, a complex application example of a FPGA-based cryptographic accelerator will be presented. In contrast to both previous examples, which focused on modelling time, control flow, and hardware / software co-design, this case study will highlight the integration of a SynDEVS model into an existing heterogeneous system.

6.3.1 Design Principles

In [Lau09], a flexible hardware / software co-processor architecture is presented which will be exploited as a foundation for the cryptographic accelerator. Please note that the presented cryptographic accelerator will only support RSA [RSA02] and ECC [Mil86, Kob87] for simplicity but could be easily extended to further provide PBC[5] support. The hardware / software co-design of the architecture was derived from the different abstraction levels of public key cryptography depicted by Figure 6.7, and, thus, the design principles of this flexible architecture are as follows [LMR+08, Lau09]:

1. Parallelization is exploited on different levels of abstraction to minimize the latency and maximize the throughput of the system. For instance, on the higher levels of abstraction, multiple cryptographic scheme operations (e.g. public key sign or verify) may be executed in parallel. Sim-

---

[5] *Pairing-Based Cryptography*

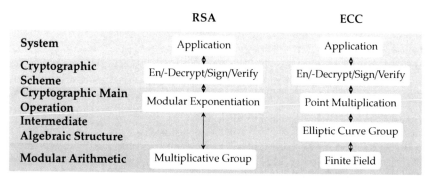

	RSA	ECC
System	Application	Application
Cryptographic Scheme	En/-Decrypt/Sign/Verify	En/-Decrypt/Sign/Verify
Cryptographic Main Operation	Modular Exponentiation	Point Multiplication
Intermediate Algebraic Structure		Elliptic Curve Group
Modular Arithmetic	Multiplicative Group	Finite Field

Figure 6.7 Abstraction level for public-key cryptography[LMR+08]

ilarly, on the lower levels of abstraction, multiple finite field arithmetic operations (e.g. modular multiplication) may be exploited in parallel.

2. Cryptographic schemes significantly differ from each other and, thus, are implemented as software for flexibility. Even more, hardware resources are saved: If the schemes would have been implemented in hardware only, then each scheme would require a single finite state machine to execute the behaviour. Thus, only a single FSM would be running at each point in time, while the others would stay unused but still consume costly hardware resources.

3. Modular operations exploited by the cryptographic schemes are very similar and, thus, will be implemented in hardware. They will be used by the software parts of the system for the calculation of the cryptographic schemes.

4. Some public key schemes need auxiliary functions (e.g. hash value generation) which are required but not often used during the overall execution time. Thus, only a single IP core will be exploited for the auxiliary functions which has to be shared between all cryptographic schemes.

In order to demonstrate its advantages, an exploitation of the SynDEVS MoC for the cryptographic main operations was chosen for the developed cryptographic accelerator. By doing so, the abstraction level of these operations remain on a high abstract level (i.e. the flexibility will be preserved) but their SynDEVS model may be transformed to hardware for a faster cryptographic scheme execution.

Figure 6.8 Initial concept of a SynDEVS model of the cryptographic accelerator

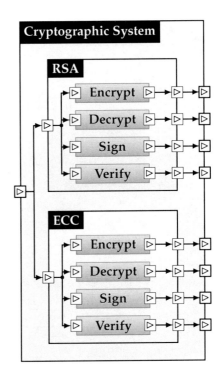

6.3.2 Architecture of the Cryptographic System

The complete cryptographic system may be modelled within SynDEVS MoC. Thus, the system designer may start with a monolithic model which may be used for design space exploration and hardware / software co-design. In Figure 6.8, a basic monolithic model of the cryptographic accelerator is illustrated. Input of the system are the cryptographic parameters (e.g. private key and plain text to be encrypted) and the type of cryptographic scheme (e.g. ECC encrypt) to be executed. The cryptographic schemes are directly implemented as atomic components. However, such an architecture is very inefficient in terms of resource utilization. Whenever a cryptographic scheme operation is executed, the resources of the other operations are unused. Thus, the model has to be refined to feature a better resource utilization.

Figure 6.9 depicts such a refined model: The cryptographic scheme operations will exploit shared components for their calculations. For instance, all cryptographic main operations (e.g. point multiplications within ECC)

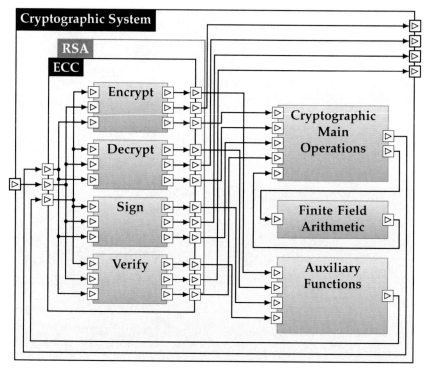

Figure 6.9 Refined SynDEVS model of the cryptographic accelerator

are moved to an independent component. By doing so, each exploited cryptographic main operation will consume resources only once and, thus, regardless of how often the operation is used within the cryptographic schemes. Furthermore, all finite field arithmetic operations may be extracted to a single atomic component. Thus, resource consumption of RSA and ECC will be further decreased. Please note that Figure 6.9 depicts only ECC but not RSA for space reasons.

The existing source code from [Mol08] to calculate the cryptographic scheme operations was exploited to preserve the flexibility of the cryptographic system in terms of maintainability or to allow the easy implementation of additional cryptographic schemes based on finite field arithmetic (e.g. PBC). Thus, the execution of the cryptographic schemes were offloaded to a MicroBlaze soft-core processor exploiting a SynDEVS model which implements the cryptographic main operations. Furthermore, to

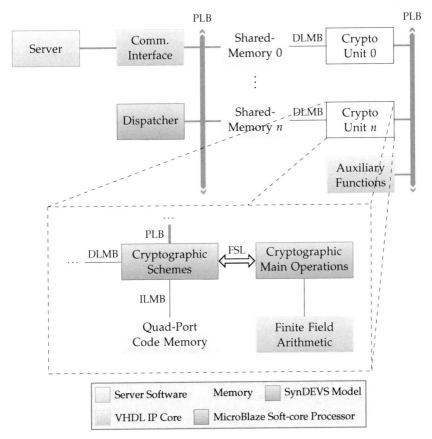

Figure 6.10 Final system architecture of the cryptographic accelerator

achieve a fast runtime of the cryptographic algorithms, the hand-optimized IP core implementing the required finite field arithmetic from [LMR$^+$08] was exploited. In contrast to the architecture from [Lau09], the cryptographic main operations (i.e. elliptic curve point doubling, point addition, and point multiplication with a scalar value) will be executed by a SynDEVS model which is very beneficial for the speed of the system.

Figure 6.10 depicts the final system architecture of the cryptographic accelerator. The server software requests the execution of cryptographic schemes (i.e. ECC signature generation) from the cryptographic accelerator. The *Dispatcher* allocates the available cryptographic units, which will perform the requested cryptographic operations, and binds them to the request. After a request binding is established, all required cryptographic parameters will be directly stored in the shared memory of the cryptographic unit. After the data was uploaded to the cryptographic unit, the dispatcher starts the requested operation. Therefore, the MicroBlaze soft-core processor of the cryptographic unit performs the requested cryptographic scheme (e.g. RSA signature generation) in software. Hence, all cryptographic main operations will be computed by a dedicated SynDEVS model implemented in hardware. To compute these operations, the SynDEVS model exploits a hand-written and optimized finite field arithmetic IP core which is implemented in hardware, too.

Please note that the software of the cryptographic scheme operations are stored in a quad-port BRAM memory. Thus, each four MicroBlaze processors share the same code memory which significantly reduces the amount of required BRAM (i.e. the bottleneck of the system). Such a quad-port BRAM has to be manually implemented by exploiting a dual-port BRAM memory with a doubled clock rate compared to the MicroBlaze processors. Then, each data port of the memory may be multiplexed to two different MicroBlaze processors by providing the port over an latch to the first MicroBlaze during the first half of the memory clock period and, afterwards, it will be latched to the second MicroBlaze during the last half of the clock period.

Please note that cryptographic scheme operations may be performed in parallel by the cryptographic units. Each cryptographic unit is completely independent and, thus, each cryptographic scheme operation may be executed for different cryptographic systems (i.e. ECC or RSA) or for different parameters (e.g. ECC 256 bit curve and RSA with a 2048 bit key). Thus, the cryptographic accelerator has a great degree of freedom regarding its application field.

After the computation of the cryptographic scheme operation is finished, the *Dispatcher* will be informed. Then, the results may be transferred back to the requesting software running on the server.

6.3.3 SynDEVS Model of the Cryptographic Main Operations

Figure 6.11 depicts the SynDEVS model for the ECC cryptographic main operations. The cryptographic schemes running as software on a MicroBlaze soft-core processor will exploit the hardware implementation of the SynDEVS model for the evaluation of elliptic curve point doubling, point

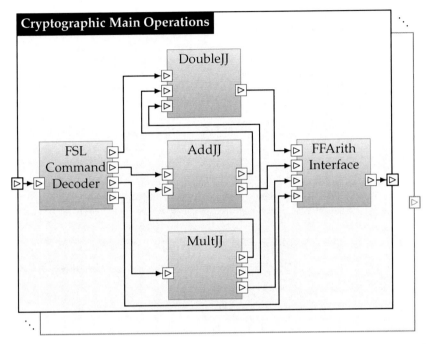

Figure 6.11 SynDEVS model for the ECC cryptographic main operations which will be exploited in parallel

addition, and point multiplication with a scalar value. Thus, the Micro-Blaze processor may send an request over FSL to the SynDEVS model to perform these operations. These requests are decoded by the *FSL Command Decoder* and forwarded to component which it belongs to. Additionally, the decoder will block the FSL of the MicroBlaze processor until the end of the requested operation.

The atomic component *DoubleJJ* calculates the ECC point doubling. Therefore, the hand-written VHDL IP core for the finite field arithmetic from [LMR+08] is exploited. To use this IP core, the *DoubleJJ* component requests different finite field operations from the *FFArith Interface* component which controls the VHDL IP core. This IP core features an internal BRAM which stores all operands of these operations and, thus, the finite field operation will solely operate on these operand registers. Specifically, the following finite field arithmetic operations may be executed: Addition, subtraction, division by two, and multiplication. Note that two finite field

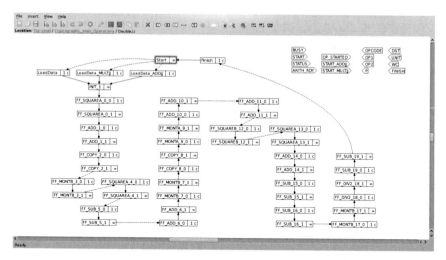

Figure 6.12 Screenshot of the *DoubleJJ* atomic component implementing the ECC double operation

multiplications may be run in parallel to further speed up the cryptographic main operations. Additionally, the VHDL IP core provides compare and copy operations.

The *DoubleJJ* component is depicted in Figure 6.12. Basically, the component state space resembles the data-flow of the ECC point doubling operation with two parallel multipliers from [Mol08]. Every two states represent a single finite field arithmetic operation: Firstly, the operation execution is requested by sending an event to the *FFArith Interface* component and secondly, the wait state with $\tau(s) = \infty$ waits for the completion of the requested operation. Hence, some multiplication operations' wait state will only wait until the requested operation is acknowledged and, afterwards, the other multiplication will be be executed in parallel to the first one. Thus, the wait state of the second multiplication operation will wait until both operations are finished.

The SynDEVS atomic component *AddJJ* calculates the ECC point addition. A special case of the ECC point addition is the addition of the same point. Then, the implemented ECC point addition algorithm would not calculate the correct output and, thus, whenever the same point should be added to itself the ECC point doubling operation will be executed instead. In addition to this preliminary operand check of the ECC point addition

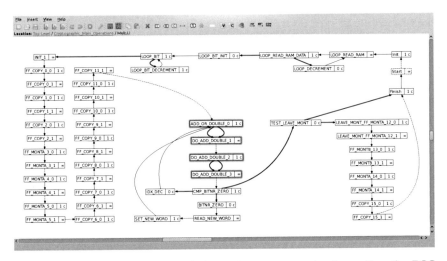

Figure 6.13 Screenshot of the *MultJJ* atomic component implementing the ECC scalar point multiplication

implementation, the rest of the component follows the implementation method of the ECC point doubling component. However, the SynDEVS representation of the implementation for the data-flow of the ECC point addition algorithm is not depicted here for brevity because it is far more complex (i.e. 129 state and 139 transitions) compared to the ECC point doubling or scalar point multiplication components.

ECC point multiplication with a scalar value will be evaluated by the *MultJJ* component. The multiplication will be performed by the basic binary schoolbook method (i.e. [HMV04, pp. 242]) and, thus, the *MultJJ* will perform a series of point addition operations and point doubling operations as a function of the scalar value's bits. Figure 6.13 depicts the *MultJJ* atomic component. The highlighted states will execute the point addition and point doubling operations at the *AddJJ* and *DoubleJJ* components. Please note that for each bit of the scalar both operations are performed every time and, thus, the implementation of the ECC scalar point multiplication is hardened against simple power or timing attacks [HMV04, pp. 242]. The rest of the states are loading the scalar value from the *FFArith* IP core's memory and are transforming the input and resulting ECC point coordinates of the ECC scalar point multiplication to and from Montgomery space which is required for fast finite field modular multiplication [MvOV96].

6.3.4 Results

The presented cryptographic accelerator was implemented on an Alpha
Data ADM-XRC-6T1 card [Alp10] equipped with a Xilinx Virtex-6 VLX365T
FPGA. The architecture of the cryptographic accelerator allows different degrees of freedom regarding the implementation: Firstly, a different
amount of cryptographic units may be exploited in parallel, cf. Section 6.3.2,
and secondly, the pipeline length of the finite field multiplication unit of
the exploited VHDL IP core may be varied, cf. [LMR+08]. Hence, some
restrictions regarding the design space exists: Cryptographic units must
be instantiated four times each because of the quad-port BRAM memory
and the amount of pipeline stages must be dividable by two. Thus, implementations for 4, 8, 12, and 16 cores and 2 up to 16 pipeline stages
were synthesized. The amount of instantiated FPGA hardware multipliers (i.e. DSP48E) scales linearly with the amount of pipeline stages and, thus,
some variants could not be implemented on the exploited FPGA because
of over-mapped resources. Therefore, the implementation variants with
four cryptographic units may include 2, 4, 6, 8, 10, 12, 14, and 16 pipeline
stages. Eight cryptographic units may exploit the pipeline with 2, 4, 6,
and 8 stages. The variants with 12 and 16 cores may only use a pipeline
with a length of 2 and 4. Taken all these different variants into account,
16 implementations of the cryptographic accelerator were synthesized and
analysed in terms of speed and resource consumption. Please note that
only the cryptographic scheme operations for ECC signature generation
and signature validation are considered in the latter for brevity. However, the presented cryptographic accelerator exploiting a SynDEVS model
is still able to compute the discussed encryption and decryption schemes
and signature generation and validation schemes for both ECC and RSA
from [LMR+08].

   Table 6.3 depicts the resource consumptions for the different implementation variants of the cryptographic accelerator. Different clock rates could
be achieved depending on the design's complexity. For instance, the implementations exploiting 16 cores could only achieve a clock rate of 100 MHz.
In contrast, the implementation variants with 4 cores could achieve clock
rates of 125 MHz and 133.$\overline{3}$ MHz. Please note that some implementation
variants featuring less resources or less complexity may achieve a slower
clock rate in comparison to the other ones, because of the synthesis tools
exploited implementation heuristics. Thus, the implementation variant
with 12 cores and a finite field arithmetic IP core pipeline length of 2 could

Table 6.3 Resource consumption of the cryptographic accelerator for the different implementation variants

Cores	Stages[b]	Registers	LUTs	Occupied Slices[a]	Clock Rate[c]
4	2	15,585 (3%)	23,447 (10%)	8,135 (14%)	133.33
4	4	18,497 (4%)	28,317 (12%)	9,811 (17%)	125.00
4	6	21,425 (4%)	33,677 (14%)	11,532 (20%)	125.00
4	8	24,353 (5%)	38,606 (16%)	12,801 (22%)	133.33
4	10	27,217 (5%)	43,397 (19%)	14,675 (26%)	133.33
4	12	30,129 (6%)	48,504 (21%)	16,258 (29%)	133.33
4	14	33,041 (7%)	53,904 (23%)	17,852 (31%)	133.33
4	16	86,008 (18%)	72,001 (31%)	32,852 (58%)	125.00
8	2	29,281 (6%)	43,808 (19%)	14,920 (26%)	125.00
8	4	35,105 (7%)	53,594 (23%)	17,992 (32%)	133.33
8	6	40,961 (9%)	64,102 (28%)	21,815 (39%)	133.33
8	8	46,817 (10%)	73,820 (32%)	24,398 (43%)	133.33
12	2	42,976 (9%)	64,152 (28%)	21,841 (39%)	133.33
12	4	51,712 (11%)	78,981 (34%)	26,054 (46%)	133.33
16	2	55,682 (12%)	83,454 (36%)	27,747 (49%)	100.00
16	4	67,330 (14%)	102,990 (45%)	34,123 (61%)	100.00

[a] Includes additional routing resources required to meet timing.
[b] Number of pipeline stages used within the finite field modular multiplier.
[c] Clock rate of the SynDEVS model.

achieve a clock rate of 133.$\overline{3}$ MHz but, in contrast, the more basic version with 8 cores and 2 pipeline stages could only reach a clock rate of 125 MHz. Hence, the very complex implementation variant with 4 cores and a 16 pipeline stages, could only be synthesized by enabling more sophisticated timing-related synthesis options (i.e. register duplication for register fan-out). Thus, this variant features a very high resource consumption in comparison to the other implementation variants with 4 cores.

Table 6.5 depicts the throughput of the system for ECC signature generation and signature validation for the NIST prime field curves [Nat99] with bit widths of 192, 224, 256, 384, and 521. For each curve's domain parameters, both, the ECDSA[6] signature generation and signature validation algorithms [Nat09, pp. 26] were executed for 10 seconds each. Then, the

---

[6] *Elliptic Curve Digital Signature Algorithm*

a) NIST P-192   b) NIST P-521

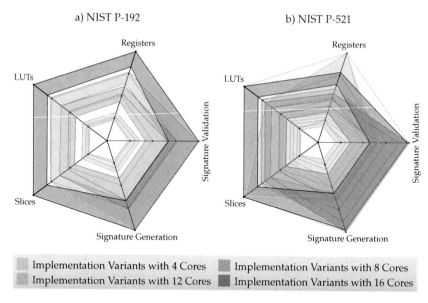

Figure 6.14 Comparison of the different implementation variants in terms of resource consumption and ECDSA algorithm throughput for the NIST P-192 and P-521 curves

number of algorithm executions per seconds were calculated for the complete system (i.e. exploiting all cryptographic units in parallel). In contrast, Table 6.6 depicts the latency of a single core for ECC signature generation and signature validation.

Figure 6.14 summarizes the figures of merit of the different implementation variants executing the ECDSA algorithms over the NIST P-192 and P-521 ECC curves. On the left hand side, the implementation variants are depicted which are able to execute the ECDSA signature generation and signature validation algorithms for the NIST P-192 curve[7]. All implementation variants with the same amount of exploited cores are grouped together and are shown by a coloured area. Each axis is scaled to the highest value found within the different implementation variants which allows a comparison of the implementation variants to each other. For instance, the 16 core variants perform similar to the 12 core variants regarding the

---

[7] The finite field arithmetic IP core is not able to operate on curves with a small bit width if a pipeline with many stages is exploited [LMR+08].

Table 6.4 Speed-up of the cryptographic accelerator exploiting a Syn-DEVS model for the cryptographic main operations

NIST Curve	Signature Generation			Signature Validation		
	P-192	P-224	P-256	P-192	P-224	P-256
This work	324.75	215.49	152.52	177.44	115.61	81.29
[Lau09]	254.19	171.61	120.92	135.84	91.73	64.91
Speed-up	27.8%	25.6%	26.1%	30.6%	26.0%	25.2%

signature generation and signature validation throughputs. However, the 16 core variants require considerably more resources than the 12 core variants. Another interesting information may be easily identified: The fast 8 core variant and the slow 12 core variant require similar resources but the 8 core variant performs better regarding ECDSA signature operation throughputs. On the right hand side, the implementation variants are depicted for the NIST P-521 curve. All implementation variants are able to operate on this large ECC curve and, thus, the figure of merit of all 16 implementation variants are shown. The implementation variant with 8 cores and 8 pipeline stages performs best for both signature generation and signature validation. Even more, this variant requires only approx. $\frac{3}{4}$ of the resources compared to the fastest implementation variant of the 16 core ones.

In comparison to the work done by [Lau09], the cryptographic accelerator exploiting a SynDEVS model for the cryptographic main operations exhibits a better performance in terms of throughput and single core latency. Table 6.4 depicts an average speed-up of approx. 27% of the SynDEVS-enabled implementation compared to the original cryptographic accelerator. However, this better performance comes with the cost of additional implementation costs. To transform the SynDEVS model to hardware, 5 components with 253 states and 283 transitions have to implemented which require additional 1,120 registers and 1,166 LUTs for each cryptographic unit in comparison to an implementation without a SynDEVS model for the cryptographic main operations (i.e. the plain software implementation of the operations from [Lau09]).

Table 6.5 Throughput of the ECC signature generation and signature validation for the different implementation variants of the cryptographic accelerator

Cores	Stages[a]	Signature Generation [ops / sec]					Signature Validation [ops / sec]				
		P-192	P-224	P-256	P-384	P-521	P-192	P-224	P-256	P-384	P-521
4	2	324.75	215.49	152.52	50.70	20.25	174.44	115.61	81.29	27.19	10.82
4	4	454.37	288.40	228.07	81.48	32.79	243.79	154.61	121.36	43.64	17.49
4	6	521.86	326.41	259.86	105.20	44.68	279.89	174.94	138.20	56.29	23.81
4	8	–	–	321.78	129.43	53.63	–	–	171.62	69.30	28.74
4	10	–	–	–	125.90	61.34	–	–	–	67.52	32.64
4	12	–	–	–	148.07	71.63	–	–	–	79.05	38.08
4	14	–	–	–	–	70.16	–	–	–	–	37.30
4	16	–	–	–	–	64.47	–	–	–	–	34.27
8	2	608.82	403.98	285.99	95.06	37.97	322.80	216.32	152.40	51.09	20.31
8	4	967.08	614.38	485.87	173.73	69.92	512.30	328.88	258.59	93.23	37.34
8	6	1,110.29	695.25	553.51	224.26	95.28	587.91	372.09	294.43	120.23	50.82
8	8	–	–	642.96	258.76	107.25	–	–	342.84	138.35	57.12
12	2	972.53	645.70	457.18	152.05	60.74	514.22	346.27	244.54	81.82	32.51
12	4	1,448.63	920.79	728.32	260.52	104.88	764.95	493.43	389.03	140.00	56.06
16	2	974.75	646.81	457.83	152.16	60.76	516.28	346.05	243.83	81.75	32.58
16	4	1,453.63	923.06	729.96	260.84	104.95	768.63	493.41	388.05	139.91	56.18

[a] Number of pipeline stages used within the finite field modular multiplier.

Table 6.6 Single core latency of the ECC signature generation and signature validation for the different implementation variants of the cryptographic accelerator

Cores	Stages[a]	Signature Generation [ms]					Signature Validation [ms]				
		P-192	P-224	P-256	P-384	P-521	P-192	P-224	P-256	P-384	P-521
4	2	12.32	18.56	26.23	78.90	197.54	22.93	34.60	49.21	147.11	369.67
4	4	8.80	13.87	17.54	49.09	122.00	16.41	25.87	32.96	91.66	228.66
4	6	7.66	12.25	15.39	38.02	89.53	14.29	22.86	28.94	71.05	168.01
4	8	–	–	12.43	30.90	74.58	–	–	23.31	57.72	139.16
4	10	–	–	–	31.77	65.21	–	–	–	59.24	122.54
4	12	–	–	–	27.01	55.85	–	–	–	50.60	105.05
4	14	–	–	–	–	57.02	–	–	–	–	107.23
4	16	–	–	–	–	62.04	–	–	–	–	116.71
8	2	13.14	19.80	27.97	84.15	210.70	24.78	36.98	52.49	156.60	393.97
8	4	8.27	13.02	16.47	46.05	114.41	15.62	24.32	30.94	85.81	214.23
8	6	7.21	11.51	14.45	35.67	83.96	13.61	21.50	27.17	66.54	157.42
8	8	–	–	12.44	30.92	74.59	–	–	23.33	57.82	140.07
12	2	12.34	18.58	26.25	78.92	197.56	23.34	34.66	49.07	146.66	369.07
12	4	8.28	13.03	16.48	46.06	114.42	15.69	24.32	30.85	85.72	214.06
16	2	16.41	24.74	34.95	105.16	263.32	30.99	46.24	65.62	195.72	491.09
16	4	11.01	17.33	21.92	61.34	152.46	20.82	32.43	41.23	114.36	284.80

[a] Number of pipeline stages used within the finite field modular multiplier.

CHAPTER 7

Summary

A hardware / software co-design flow for the SynDEVS MoC was presented in this thesis. The SynDEVS MoC was introduced which is a revised version of the time-discrete DEVS formalism from Zeigler et al. It was reviewed in detail in terms of synthesis aspects in contrast to the non-synthesizable DEVS MoC. Understanding the behaviour of SynDEVS models was boosted by declaring a visual representation in favour of the more formal pure mathematical notation. This visual programming paradigm was further extended by developing a GUI which allows for the creation of models. By doing so, all intermediate models of the co-design flow may be reviewed from within the GUI.

The advocated abstract system level design flow, which allows for transformation of a such a timed MoC into into synthesizable VHDL source code and embeddable C++ source code, is the main contribution of this thesis. Both transformation paths from the SynDEVS MoC to hardware and software instances were discussed in detail. A state optimization algorithm for the DEVS MoC's zero-timeout states, which is an inherent property of the DEVS MoC to model conditional execution within a single step in time, was introduced. A dedicated application example, the DVI controller, enabled the demonstration of the important steps within the design flow in order to relax the timing requirements of the synthesised model. Besides that, this illustrative example shows the effectiveness of the hardware transformation methodology regarding synthesis of a model with strict timing-requirements.

To allow an efficient use of the hardware / software co-design, the communication in between the hardware and software parts were automatically generated in terms of a proof-of-concept FSL interface link. It was emphasized that a successful introduction of MoCs into the development of embedded systems requires the possibility to include legacy software libraries. A dedicated SynDEVS component was introduced to allow the reuse of such legacy software libraries written in C / C++ source code. Hardware / software co-design including automated communication interface generation and legacy software inclusion was demonstrated by the means of a network-based Pong game.

However, as the development of embedded system is in general an evolutionary process, it was demonstrated that the introduction of SynDEVS MoC into an existing design is feasible: An existing hardware / software co-design of a cryptographic accelerator was enriched with a SynDEVS model for evaluation of the cryptographic main operations. Results exemplify that such a late introduction of SynDEVS MoC is highly beneficial for the figures of merit in terms of throughput.

To enable the application of the advocated design flow in further areas, it was detailed how other MoCs may be transformed into the SynDEVS MoC. Then, models from these MoCs may be exploited within the advocated system level design flow, too. Furthermore, model validation in terms of simulation with SystemC was described in detail. A non-intrusive SystemC kernel extension was developed to allow a fast simulation of the SynDEVS MoC. Nevertheless, the described transformation methodology for the hardware / software co-design of the SynDEVS MoC as well as the SystemC implementation methodology may be applicable to other time-discrete MoCs, too.

Abstract system level design with MoCs in terms of SynDEVS MoC is still in its infancy. There are a many open research challenges and interesting opportunities to broaden the scope of the advocated hardware / software co-design flow. So far, only models from time-discrete domains are covered but cyber physical systems demand continuously timed models, too. Thus, it is of utmost interest to expand the described methodology to cover these MoCs.

Another extension would be to expand the existing hardware / software co-design flow to feature more sophisticated design space exploration methods. Even more, an integration of reconfiguration (i.e. RecDEVS) into the lower abstraction levels of the design flow would be interesting and will rise important questions. For instance, how can the time flow within a model preserved if reconfiguration will occur during the execution of the model, which itself needs time.

An introduction of a special purpose processing unit for SynDEVS MoC would be another interesting aspect. Then, software execution with respect to timing could be achieved more efficiently in contrast to the exploitation of an untimed software language like C++ which is a cumbersome task. Having that said, it is still useful because of the legacy software library support. Hence, exploitation of multi-core architectures on the software part of the advocated hardware / software co-design flow could be enhanced by using a RTOS[1]. Such an approach would allow the reuse of more complex legacy software libraries including those which require operation system support (e.g. task management). By doing so, the application field of abstract system level design with MoCs would be further broadened.

---

[1] *Real-time Operating System*

APPENDIX A

Source Codes

A.1 DEVS Component

Listing A.1 **DEVS_Component**\<State\> base class

```
1 template <class State> class DEVS_Component_Advance_Callback;
2 template <class State> void *run_devs_internal_transition_thread(
     void *param);
3 template <class State> void *run_devs_external_transition_thread(
     void *param);
4 template <class State> void *run_devs_confluence_transition_thread(
     void *param);
5
6 // define the debug output granularity
7 #define DBG_NONE              0x0000
8 #define DBG_ADVANCE           0x0001
9 #define DBG_DELTA             0x0002
10 #define DBG_INT_TRANSITION   0x0004
11 #define DBG_EXT_TRANSITION   0x0008
12 #define DBG_CONFLUENCE       0x0010
13 #define DBG_TIMEOUT          0x0020
14
15 // some combinations of debug flags from above
16 #define DBG_ALL              0x003F
17 #define DBG_TRANSITION       0x000C
18
19 // optimization flags
20 #define OPT_NONE             0x0000
21 #define OPT_ALL_PARALLEL     0x0001
22 #define OPT_ALL_SERIAL       0x0002
23 #define OPT_NEEDED_SERIAL    0x0004
24
25 // parallel execution flags
26 #define NONE_EXECUTED        0x0000
27 #define INT_EXECUTED         0x0001
```

```cpp
28 #define EXT_EXECUTED              0x0002
29 #define CON_EXECUTED              0x0004
30 #define ALL_EXECUTED              (INT_EXECUTED|EXT_EXECUTED|CON_EXECUTED)
31
32 // pthread mutex and condition helpers
33 #define PRE_WAIT_FOR_COND(mutex,cond) pthread_mutex_lock(&mutex);
34 #define POST_WAIT_FOR_COND(mutex,cond) pthread_cond_wait(&cond, &
      mutex);pthread_mutex_unlock(&mutex);
35 #define POST_WAIT_FOR_COND_EXECUTED(mutex,cond,signal) while (
      parallelExecutionStatus != signal) { pthread_cond_wait(&cond, &
      mutex); } pthread_mutex_unlock(&mutex);
36 #define SIGNAL_COND_EXECUTED(mutex,cond,signal) pthread_mutex_lock(&
      mutex);parallelExecutionStatus |= signal;pthread_cond_broadcast
      (&cond);pthread_mutex_unlock(&mutex);
37 #define SIGNAL_COND(mutex,cond) pthread_mutex_lock(&mutex);
      pthread_cond_broadcast(&cond);pthread_mutex_unlock(&mutex);
38
39 std::string timestamp(bool bWithDelta=false,const std::string post="
      ");
40
41 template<class State> class DEVS_Component : public sc_module {
42 public:
43   friend class DEVS_Component_Advance_Callback<State>;
44   friend void *run_devs_internal_transition_thread<State>(void *
        param);
45   friend void *run_devs_external_transition_thread<State>(void *
        param);
46   friend void *run_devs_confluence_transition_thread<State>(void *
        param);
47
48   SC_CTOR(DEVS_Component) : debugLevel(DBG_NONE) {
49     lastActive = DEVS_TIME_ZERO;
50     optimizeLevel = OPT_ALL_PARALLEL;
51     parallelExecutionStatus = NONE_EXECUTED;
52     pthread_mutex_init(&advanceConditionMutex, NULL);
53     pthread_cond_init(&advanceCondition, NULL);
54     pthread_mutex_init(&returnToAdvanceConditionMutex, NULL);
55     pthread_cond_init(&returnToAdvanceCondition, NULL);
56   }
57
58   virtual const char *devsname() const {
59     return name();
60   }
61
62   State DBGgetCurState() {
63     return curState;
64   }
65
66   void verbose(unsigned int verbosity=DBG_ADVANCE) {
```

```
67      debugLevel = verbosity;
68    }
69
70    void optimize(unsigned int opt=OPT_NEEDED_SERIAL) {
71      optimizeLevel = opt;
72    }
73
74    const void print(std::ostream& os) {
75      print(os, curState);
76    }
77
78    /*
79     * Startup the devs component.
80     */
81    void devs_startup() {
82      if (debugLevel != DBG_NONE)
83        cerr << devsname() << "_devs_startup()" << endl;
84      // make devs_advance sensitive to timeoutEvent and register the
                component's input ports
85      devs_advance_options.set_sensitivity(&timeoutEvent);
86      register_input_ports();
87      // spawn the process (started immediatly)
88      sc_spawn(DEVS_Component_Advance_Callback<State >(this),
              sc_gen_unique_name(std::string(devsname()).append("
              _devs_advance").c_str()), &devs_advance_options);
89      if (optimizeLevel&OPT_ALL_PARALLEL) {
90        pthread_create(&internalThread, NULL,
              run_devs_internal_transition_thread<State >, this);
91        pthread_create(&externalThread, NULL,
              run_devs_external_transition_thread<State >, this);
92        pthread_create(&confluenceThread, NULL,
              run_devs_confluence_transition_thread<State >, this);
93      }
94    }
95
96    // Model-generic functions
97  private:
98
99    /*
100    * Do the final initialization of the devs component.
101    * It belongs directly to the devs_startup() hence it is not
            called there because the DEVS_Component_Advance_Callback may
            not yet be started.
102    */
103   void devs_initialize() {
104     curState = initialize();
105     devs_timeout();
106   }
107
```

```
108   void devs_confluence_transition_thread(void) {
109     PRE_WAIT_FOR_COND(advanceConditionMutex, advanceCondition);
110     SIGNAL_COND_EXECUTED(returnToAdvanceConditionMutex,
            returnToAdvanceCondition, CON_EXECUTED);
111     for (;;) {
112       // wait for the signal to start the execution
113       POST_WAIT_FOR_COND(advanceConditionMutex, advanceCondition);
114       // execute the confluence transition function
115       if (debugLevel&DBG_CONFLUENCE) {
116         cout << TRANSITION() << std::setw(12) << timestamp(":_") <<
                 "[" << devsname() << "]_devs_confluence_transition_";
117         print(cout);
118       }
119       conState = confluence(curState, devs_elapsed_time());
120       if (debugLevel&DBG_CONFLUENCE) {
121         cout << "_->_";
122         print(cout, conState);
123         cout << NORMAL() << endl;
124       }
125       // signal the end of executon
126       PRE_WAIT_FOR_COND(advanceConditionMutex, advanceCondition);
127       SIGNAL_COND_EXECUTED(returnToAdvanceConditionMutex,
              returnToAdvanceCondition, CON_EXECUTED);
128     }
129   }
130
131   void devs_external_transition_thread(void) {
132     PRE_WAIT_FOR_COND(advanceConditionMutex, advanceCondition);
133     SIGNAL_COND_EXECUTED(returnToAdvanceConditionMutex,
            returnToAdvanceCondition, EXT_EXECUTED);
134     for (;;) {
135       // wait for the signal to start the execution
136       POST_WAIT_FOR_COND(advanceConditionMutex, advanceCondition);
137       // execute the external transition function
138       if (debugLevel&DBG_EXT_TRANSITION) {
139         cout << TRANSITION() << std::setw(12) << timestamp(":_") <<
                 "[" << devsname() << "]_devs_external_transition_";
140         print(cout);
141       }
142       extState = external_transition(curState, devs_elapsed_time());
143       if (debugLevel&DBG_EXT_TRANSITION) {
144         cout << "_->_";
145         print(cout, extState);
146         cout << NORMAL() << endl;
147       }
148       // signal the end of executon
149       PRE_WAIT_FOR_COND(advanceConditionMutex, advanceCondition);
150       SIGNAL_COND_EXECUTED(returnToAdvanceConditionMutex,
              returnToAdvanceCondition, EXT_EXECUTED);
```

```
151       }
152     }
153
154     void devs_internal_transition_thread(void) {
155       PRE_WAIT_FOR_COND(advanceConditionMutex, advanceCondition);
156       SIGNAL_COND_EXECUTED(returnToAdvanceConditionMutex,
                 returnToAdvanceCondition, INT_EXECUTED);
157       for (;;) {
158         // wait for the signal to start the execution
159         POST_WAIT_FOR_COND(advanceConditionMutex, advanceCondition);
160         // execute the internal transition function
161         if (debugLevel&DBG_INT_TRANSITION) {
162           cout << TRANSITION() << std::setw(12) << timestamp(":_") <<
                   "[" << devsname() << "]_devs_internal_transition_";
163           print(cout);
164         }
165         intState = internal_transition(curState);
166         if (debugLevel&DBG_INT_TRANSITION) {
167           cout << "_->_";
168           print(cout, intState);
169           cout << NORMAL() << endl;
170         }
171         // signal the end of executon
172         PRE_WAIT_FOR_COND(advanceConditionMutex, advanceCondition);
173         SIGNAL_COND_EXECUTED(returnToAdvanceConditionMutex,
                   returnToAdvanceCondition, INT_EXECUTED);
174       }
175     }
176
177     void devs_confluence_transition(void) {
178       if (debugLevel&DBG_CONFLUENCE) {
179         cout << TRANSITION() << std::setw(12) << timestamp(":_") << "[
                 " << devsname() << "]_devs_confluence_transition_";
180         print(cout);
181       }
182       conState = confluence(curState, devs_elapsed_time());
183       if (debugLevel&DBG_CONFLUENCE) {
184         cout << "_->_";
185         print(cout, conState);
186         cout << NORMAL() << endl;
187       }
188     }
189
190     void devs_external_transition(void) {
191       if (debugLevel&DBG_EXT_TRANSITION) {
192         cout << TRANSITION() << std::setw(12) << timestamp(":_") << "[
                 " << devsname() << "]_devs_external_transition_";
193         print(cout);
194       }
```

```
195     extState = external_transition(curState , devs_elapsed_time());
196     if (debugLevel&DBG_EXT_TRANSITION) {
197       cout << "_->_";
198       print(cout, extState);
199       cout << NORMAL() << endl;
200     }
201   }
202
203   void devs_internal_transition(void) {
204     if (debugLevel&DBG_INT_TRANSITION) {
205       cout << TRANSITION() << std::setw(12) << timestamp(":_") << "[
            " << devsname() << "]_devs_internal_transition_";
206       print(cout);
207     }
208     intState = internal_transition(curState);
209     if (debugLevel&DBG_INT_TRANSITION) {
210       cout << "_->_";
211       print(cout, intState);
212       cout << NORMAL() << endl;
213     }
214   }
215
216   void devs_advance(void) {
217     State nextState;
218     bool extTransitionOccured = false;   // will be true if a
              external transition occured
219     bool intTransitionOccured = false;   // will be true if a
              internal transition occured
220     std::list<devs_in_if*>::iterator it;
221     intTransitionOccured = (time_advance(curState) ==
            devs_elapsed_time());
222     // scan over all input ports and look if one got an event.
223     for (it = listInputs.begin(); (it != listInputs.end()) && !
            extTransitionOccured; it++) {
224       if ((*it)->event())
225         extTransitionOccured = true;
226     }
227     if (optimizeLevel&OPT_NEEDED_SERIAL) {
228       // serial calls to the next state functions
229       if (extTransitionOccured && intTransitionOccured) {
230         devs_confluence_transition();
231       } else if (extTransitionOccured && !intTransitionOccured) {
232         devs_external_transition();
233       } else if (intTransitionOccured && !extTransitionOccured) {
234         devs_internal_transition();
235       }
236     } else if (optimizeLevel&OPT_ALL_PARALLEL) {
237       // clear the status variable (describes which threads finished
              their execution)
```

```
238        PRE_WAIT_FOR_COND( returnToAdvanceConditionMutex ,
               returnToAdvanceCondition );
239        while (parallelExecutionStatus != ALL_EXECUTED) {
240          pthread_cond_wait(&returnToAdvanceCondition , &
               returnToAdvanceConditionMutex );
241        }
242        parallelExecutionStatus = NONE_EXECUTED;
243        // signal all threads (internal , external , confluence ) to
               start their execution
244        SIGNAL_COND( advanceConditionMutex , advanceCondition );
245        // wait for the threads to be finished
246        POST_WAIT_FOR_COND_EXECUTED( returnToAdvanceConditionMutex ,
               returnToAdvanceCondition , ALL_EXECUTED);
247      } else if (optimizeLevel&OPT_ALL_SERIAL) {
248        unsigned int call = 0x7, bit ;
249        // Shuffle the three transition calls but execute each only
               once .
250        while (call != 0) {
251          do {
252            bit = 1 << (rand()%3);
253          } while ((call&bit)==0);
254          if (bit == 0x1) {
255            devs_internal_transition ();
256          } else if (bit == 0x2) {
257            devs_external_transition ();
258          } else {
259            devs_confluence_transition ();
260          }
261          call &= ~bit ;
262        }
263      } else {
264        cerr << ERROR() << std :: setw (8) << "_###_ERROR_in_" << name()
               << ":_devs_advance()_called_without_a_correct_optimize_
               level_(no_OPT_ALL_SERIAL,_OPT_NEEDED_SERIAL,_
               OPT_ALL_PARALLEL_given)._###" << NORMAL() << endl <<
               BACKTRACE() << endl ;
265
266      }
267
268      if (extTransitionOccured && intTransitionOccured) {
269        nextState = conState ;
270      } else if (extTransitionOccured && !intTransitionOccured) {
271        nextState = extState ;
272      } else if (intTransitionOccured && !extTransitionOccured) {
273        nextState = intState ;
274      } else {
275        cerr << ERROR() << std :: setw (8) << "_###_ERROR_in_" << name()
               << ":_devs_advance()_called_without_extTransitionOccured_
               or_intTransitionOccured ._###" << NORMAL() << endl <<
```

```cpp
                   BACKTRACE() << endl;
276            nextState = initialize(); // fallback. this should never be
                   hit!
277
278        }
279
280        if (debugLevel&DBG_ADVANCE) {
281            cout << ADVANCE() << std::setw(12) << timestamp(":␣") << "["
                   << devsname() << "]␣devs_advance␣with␣int=" <<
                   intTransitionOccured << "␣and␣ext=" <<
                   extTransitionOccured << "␣␣";
282            print(cout);
283            cout << "␣=>␣";
284            print(cout, nextState);
285            cout << NORMAL() << endl;
286        }
287
288        // output data, iff an internal transition occurred
289        if (intTransitionOccured)
290            output(curState);
291
292        // update current state, update last active timestamp and set
                   the new timeout for the internal transition
293        curState = nextState;
294        devs_update_time();
295        devs_timeout();
296    }
297
298    void devs_timeout(void) {
299        devs_time next_timeout = time_advance(curState);
300        if (debugLevel&DBG_TIMEOUT) cout << TIMEOUT() << std::setw(12)
                   << timestamp(":␣") << "[" << devsname() << "]␣devs_timeout␣
                   ->␣" << next_timeout << NORMAL() << endl;
301
302        timeoutEvent.cancel();
303        if (next_timeout != DEVS_TIME_INF) {
304            timeoutEvent.notify(next_timeout.get_sc_time());
305        }
306    }
307
308    devs_core::devs_time devs_elapsed_time(void) {
309        return sc_time_stamp() - lastActive;
310    }
311    void devs_update_time(void) {
312        lastActive = sc_time_stamp();
313    }
314
315    std::string timestamp(const std::string post="") {
316        return devs_core::timestamp((debugLevel& DBG_DELTA)!=0, post);
```

```
317    }
318
319  protected :
320      mutable sc_spawn_options devs_advance_options; // used to save the
               sensitivity of the component for the input port(s)
321      void register_input(devs_in_if *in_if) const {
322         devs_advance_options.set_sensitivity(&(in_if->default_event()));
323         listInputs.push_back(in_if);
324      }
325
326      // Model-specific functions
327  protected :
328      virtual void print(std::ostream& os, const State& state) const =0;
329      virtual void register_input_ports(void) const =0;
330      virtual State initialize(void) const =0;
331      virtual void output(const State& state) const =0;
332      virtual devs_core::devs_time time_advance(const State& state)
               const =0;
333      virtual State external_transition(const State& state, const
               devs_core::devs_time& elapsed) const =0;
334      virtual State internal_transition(const State& state) const =0;
335      virtual State confluence(const State& state, const devs_core::
               devs_time& elapsed) const =0;
336
337  private :
338      pthread_mutex_t advanceConditionMutex,
               returnToAdvanceConditionMutex; // Mutex to synchronize the
               access to the conditions below.
339      pthread_cond_t advanceCondition, returnToAdvanceCondition; //
               Conditions between {int,ext,con}-Transition and devs_advance.
340      pthread_t externalThread, internalThread, confluenceThread; // The
               threads for the parallel version.
341      unsigned int parallelExecutionStatus; // Current status of the
               parallel executed threads, i.e. which is currently runnning.
342      unsigned int optimizeLevel; // Flags to indicate that the parallel
               next state calls should be serial calls.
343      State curState; // the current state of the devs;
344      State extState; // the next state after the external transition
345      State intState; // the next state after the internal transition
346      State conState; // the next state after the confluence transition
347      // (both internal and external events fired up the component)
348      devs_core::devs_time lastActive; // hold the timestamp the last
               transition occured
349      sc_event timeoutEvent; // event for the timeout of a state (fires
               internal_transition)
350      mutable std::list <devs_core::devs_in_if*> listInputs; // this list
               saves a reference to all used (registered) input ports
351      unsigned int debugLevel; // debug output is appreciated with
               verbosity 0=none,1=essential,2=all
```

```
352 };
353
354 template <class State> std::ostream& operator << (std::ostream& os,
        DEVS_Component<State>& component) {
355   component.print(os);
356   return os;
357 };
358
359 template <class State> void *run_devs_external_transition_thread(
        void *param) {
360   DEVS_Component<State> *model = (DEVS_Component<State>*)param;
361   model->devs_external_transition_thread();
362   return NULL;
363 }
364
365 template <class State> void *run_devs_internal_transition_thread(
        void *param) {
366   DEVS_Component<State> *model = (DEVS_Component<State>*)param;
367   model->devs_internal_transition_thread();
368   return NULL;
369 }
370
371 template <class State> void *run_devs_confluence_transition_thread(
        void *param) {
372   DEVS_Component<State> *model = (DEVS_Component<State>*)param;
373   model->devs_confluence_transition_thread();
374   return NULL;
375 }
376
377 template <class State> class DEVS_Component_Advance_Callback {
378 public:
379   DEVS_Component_Advance_Callback(DEVS_Component<State>* target) {
380     target_p = target;
381   }
382   inline void operator () () {
383     target_p->devs_initialize();
384     while (true) {
385       wait();
386       target_p->devs_advance();
387     }
388   }
389 protected:
390   DEVS_Component<State>* target_p;
391 };
```

A.2 GPT Example

Listing A.2 Generator component

```
1  STATE_SET(Phase);
2  STATE(Phase, WAIT);
3  STATE(Phase, GENERATE);
4
5  struct GeneratorState {
6    Phase phase;
7    unsigned int count;
8    devs_time period;
9  };
10
11 class Generator : public DEVS_Component<GeneratorState> {
12 public:
13   DEVS_OUT<unsigned int> iOutput;
14   DEVS_IN<unsigned int> iStart;
15   DEVS_IN<unsigned int> iStop;
16   devs_time initPeriod;
17
18   Generator(sc_module_name name, devs_time _initPeriod) :
         DEVS_Component<GeneratorState >(name) {
19     initPeriod = _initPeriod;
20   };
21
22   virtual void register_input_ports(void) const {
23     register_input(&iStart);
24     register_input(&iStop);
25   }
26
27   GeneratorState initialize(void) const {
28     GeneratorState ret = {WAIT, 0, DEVS_TIME_INF};
29     return ret;
30   }
31
32   void output(const GeneratorState& state) const {
33     iOutput = state.count;
34   }
35
36   devs_time time_advance(const GeneratorState& state) const {
37     return state.period;
38   }
39
40   GeneratorState external_transition(const GeneratorState& state,
         const devs_time& elapsed) const {
41     if (state.phase == WAIT && iStart == 1) {
```

```
42      GeneratorState next_state;
43      next_state.phase = GENERATE;
44      next_state.count = state.count;
45      next_state.period  = initPeriod;
46      return next_state;
47    } else if (state.phase == GENERATE && iStop == 1) {
48      GeneratorState next_state;
49      next_state.phase = WAIT;
50      next_state.count = state.count;
51      next_state.period  = DEVS_TIME_INF;
52      return next_state;
53    }
54    return state;
55  }
56
57  GeneratorState internal_transition(const GeneratorState& state)
        const {
58    GeneratorState next_state;
59
60    next_state = state;
61    next_state.count++;
62
63    return next_state;
64  }
65
66  GeneratorState confluence(const GeneratorState& state, const
        devs_time& elapsed) const {
67    return external_transition(internal_transition(state), elapsed);
68  }
69 };
```

Listing A.3 Process component

```
1 STATE_SET(Processor);
2 STATE(Processor, WAITFORJOB);
3 STATE(Processor, PROCESS);
4
5 struct ProcessorState {
6   Processor phase;
7   unsigned int count;
8   devs_time period;
9 };
10
11 class Processor : public DEVS_Component<ProcessorState> {
12 public:
13   DEVS_OUT<unsigned int> iOutput;
14   DEVS_IN<unsigned int> iInput;
15   devs_time initPeriod;
```

```
16
17    Processor(sc_module_name name, devs_time _initPeriod) :
         DEVS_Component<ProcessorState >(name) {
18      initPeriod = _initPeriod;
19    };
20
21    virtual void register_input_ports(void) const {
22      register_input(&iInput);
23    }
24
25    ProcessorState initialize(void) const {
26      ProcessorState ret = {WAITFORJOB, 0, DEVS_TIME_INF};
27      return ret;
28    }
29
30    void output(const ProcessorState& state) const {
31      iOutput = state.count;
32    }
33
34    devs_time time_advance(const ProcessorState& state) const {
35      return state.period;
36    }
37
38    ProcessorState external_transition(const ProcessorState& state,
         const devs_time& elapsed) const {
39      ProcessorState next_state = state;
40      if (state.phase == WAITFORJOB) {
41        next_state.phase = PROCESS;
42        next_state.count = iInput;
43        next_state.period = initPeriod;
44        return next_state;
45      }
46      next_state.period -= elapsed;
47      return next_state;
48    }
49
50    ProcessorState internal_transition(const ProcessorState& state)
         const {
51      return initialize();
52    }
53
54    ProcessorState confluence(const ProcessorState& state, const
         devs_time& elapsed) const {
55      return external_transition(internal_transition(state), elapsed);
56    }
57
58 };
```

Listing A.4 Observer component

```
 1 STATE_SET(Observer);
 2 STATE(Observer, OBSERVE);
 3 STATE(Observer, END);
 4
 5 struct ObserverState {
 6   Observer phase;
 7   unsigned int in, out;
 8   devs_time period;
 9 };
10
11 class Observer : public DEVS_Component<ObserverState> {
12 public:
13   DEVS_IN<unsigned int> iJobStart;
14   DEVS_IN<unsigned int> iJobStop;
15   DEVS_OUT<unsigned int> iStopGenerator;
16   devs_time initPeriod;
17
18   Observer(sc_module_name name, devs_time _initPeriod) :
          DEVS_Component<ObserverState>(name) {
19     initPeriod = _initPeriod;
20   };
21
22   virtual void register_input_ports(void) const {
23     register_input(&iJobStart);
24     register_input(&iJobStop);
25   }
26
27   ObserverState initialize(void) const {
28     ObserverState ret = {OBSERVE, 0, 0, initPeriod};
29     return ret;
30   }
31
32   void output(const ObserverState& state) const {
33     iStopGenerator = 1;
34   }
35
36   devs_time time_advance(const ObserverState& state) const {
37     return state.period;
38   }
39
40   ObserverState external_transition(const ObserverState& state,
          const devs_time& elapsed) const {
41     ObserverState next_state = state;
42     if (state.phase == OBSERVE) {
43       if (iJobStart.event())
44         next_state.in++;
45       if (iJobStop.event())
```

```
46            next_state.out++;
47          next_state.period -= elapsed;
48        }
49      return next_state;
50    }
51
52    ObserverState internal_transition(const ObserverState& state)
          const {
53      ObserverState next_state=state;
54      next_state.phase = END;
55      next_state.period = DEVS_TIME_INF;
56      return next_state;
57    }
58
59    ObserverState confluence(const ObserverState& state, const
          devs_time& elapsed) const {
60      return external_transition(internal_transition(state), elapsed);
61    }
62  };
```

Listing A.5 sc_main function implementing the *gpt* example

```
1  int sc_main(int argc, char* argv[]) {
2    devs_signal<unsigned int> gen_out;
3    devs_signal<unsigned int> proc_obs;
4    devs_signal<unsigned int> obs_gen;
5    devs_signal<unsigned int> tb_out;
6    unsigned int g=1,p=1,t=10000;
7
8    Generator generator("Generator", devs_time(g, SC_NS));
9    generator.optimize(OPT_NEEDED_SERIAL);
10   generator.iStart(tb_out);
11   generator.iStop(obs_gen);
12   generator.iOutput(gen_out);
13
14   Processor processor("Processor", devs_time(p, SC_NS));
15   processor.optimize(OPT_NEEDED_SERIAL);
16   processor.iInput(gen_out);
17   processor.iOutput(proc_obs);
18
19   Observer observer("Observer", devs_time(t, SC_NS));
20   observer.optimize(OPT_NEEDED_SERIAL);
21   observer.iJobStart(gen_out);
22   observer.iJobStop(proc_obs);
23   observer.iStopGenerator(obs_gen);
24
25   // initialize model and run it
26   generator.devs_startup();
```

```
27    processor.devs_startup();
28    observer.devs_startup();
29    sc_start();
30
31    return(0);
32 }
```

A.3 UART Receiver (VHDL)

Listing A.6 UART Receiver VHDL source code automatically generated from the SynDEVS model

```vhdl
1 library IEEE;
2 use IEEE.NUMERIC_BIT.ALL;
3 library devs_uart_v1_00_a;
4 use devs_uart_v1_00_a.FUNCTIONS.ALL;
5
6 entity RECEIVER is
7   generic(
8     timer_width: integer := 10;
9     default_value: integer := 0
10  );
11  port(
12    clk: in bit;
13    reset: in bit;
14    rx: in bit;
15    rx_enable: in bit;
16    data_received: out unsigned(7 downto 0);
17    data_received_enable: out bit;
18    data_error: out bit;
19    data_error_enable: out bit;
20    timer_stop_in: in bit;
21    disable_in: in bit
22  );
23 end entity;
24
25 architecture BEHAVIOURAL of RECEIVER is
26   type states_type is (state_idle, state_startbit,
            state_waitforfirstbit, state_readbit, state_parity,
            state_waitstopbit);
27   signal state: states_type := state_idle;
28   signal data: unsigned(7 downto 0) := TO_UNSIGNED(0,8);
29   signal bitsread: unsigned(3 downto 0) := TO_UNSIGNED(0,4);
30   signal evenparity: bit := '0';
31   signal stop: bit := '0';
32   signal timer: unsigned(timer_width - 1 downto 0) := TO_UNSIGNED(
            default_value, timer_width);
33 begin
34   RECEIVER: process(clk, reset) is
35   begin
36     if (reset = '0') then
37       if (clk'event and clk = '1') then
38         if (timer_stop_in = '0') then
39           timer <= devs_uart_v1_00_a.FUNCTIONS.decrement(timer);
```

```vhdl
40          end if;
41          if (timer=TO_UNSIGNED(0,timer_width)) then
42            timer <= TO_UNSIGNED(default_value,timer_width);
43          end if;
44          if (disable_in='1') then
45            data_received_enable <= '0';
46            data_error_enable <= '0';
47          end if;
48          case (state) is
49            when state_idle =>
50              if (disable_in='1' and rx='0' and rx_enable='1') then
51                timer <= TO_UNSIGNED(433,10);
52                state <= state_startbit;
53              end if;
54            when state_startbit =>
55              if (TIMER /= TO_UNSIGNED(0,timer_width) and disable_in
                    ='1' and rx='1' and rx_enable='1') then
56                state <= state_idle;
57              end if;
58              if (disable_in='1' and TIMER=TO_UNSIGNED(0,timer_width)
                    and rx='0' and rx_enable='1') then
59                timer <= TO_UNSIGNED(867,10);
60                data <= TO_UNSIGNED(0,8);
61                bitsread <= TO_UNSIGNED(0,4);
62                evenparity <= '0';
63                stop <= '0';
64                state <= state_waitforfirstbit;
65              end if;
66            when state_waitforfirstbit =>
67              if (disable_in='1' and TIMER=TO_UNSIGNED(0,timer_width)
                    and rx_enable='1') then
68                timer <= TO_UNSIGNED(867,10);
69                data <= rx&data(7 downto 1);
70                bitsread <= bitsread+TO_UNSIGNED(1,4);
71                evenparity <= rx xor evenparity;
72                state <= state_readbit;
73              end if;
74            when state_readbit =>
75              if (disable_in='1' and TIMER=TO_UNSIGNED(0,timer_width)
                    and rx_enable='1' and (not (bitsread=TO_UNSIGNED
                    (8,4)))) then
76                timer <= TO_UNSIGNED(867,10);
77                data <= rx&data(7 downto 1);
78                bitsread <= bitsread+TO_UNSIGNED(1,4);
79                evenparity <= rx xor evenparity;
80                state <= state_readbit;
81              end if;
82              if (disable_in='1' and TIMER=TO_UNSIGNED(0,timer_width)
                    and rx_enable='1' and bitsread=TO_UNSIGNED(8,4))
```

```
                          then
83                        timer <= TO_UNSIGNED(867,10);
84                        evenparity <= rx xor evenparity;
85                        state <= state_parity;
86                      end if;
87                  when state_parity =>
88                    if (disable_in='1' and TIMER=TO_UNSIGNED(0,timer_width)
                          and rx_enable='1') then
89                        timer <= TO_UNSIGNED(433,10);
90                        stop <= rx;
91                        state <= state_waitstopbit;
92                      end if;
93                  when state_waitstopbit =>
94                    if (disable_in='1' and TIMER=TO_UNSIGNED(0,timer_width)
                          and rx_enable='1' and (stop='1' and evenparity='0'))
                          then
95                        data_received <= data;
96                        data_received_enable <= '1';
97                        state <= state_idle;
98                      end if;
99                    if (disable_in='1' and TIMER=TO_UNSIGNED(0,timer_width)
                          and rx_enable='1' and (not (stop='1' and evenparity
                          ='0'))) then
100                       data_error <= '1';
101                       data_error_enable <= '1';
102                       state <= state_idle;
103                     end if;
104               end case;
105             end if;
106         else
107           timer <= TO_UNSIGNED(default_value,timer_width);
108           state <= state_idle;
109           data  <= TO_UNSIGNED(0,8);
110           bitsread <= TO_UNSIGNED(0,4);
111           evenparity <= '0';
112           stop <= '0';
113           data_received <= (others => '0');
114           data_received_enable <= '0';
115           data_error <= '0';
116           data_error_enable <= '0';
117         end if;
118    end process RECEIVER;
119 end architecture BEHAVIOURAL;
```

A.4 UART Transceiver (C++)

Listing A.7 `Atomic_Component_transmitter` class declaration with additional declaration of the component's states

```
1 #ifndef ATOMIC_COMPONENT_TRANSMITTER_H_
2 #define ATOMIC_COMPONENT_TRANSMITTER_H_
3
4 #include "ComponentState.h"
5 #include "Atomic_Component.h"
6 #include "RegisterFile.h"
7 #include "Port.h"
8 #include "model_definitions.h"
9 #ifdef DEBUG
10    #include "xparameters.h"
11    #include "stdio.h"
12 #endif /* DEBUG */
13
14 extern RegisterFile registerFile;
15
16 // State IDS
17 #define STATE_transmitter_IDLE      1
18 #define STATE_transmitter_READDATA   2
19 #define STATE_transmitter_SENDBIT 3
20 #define STATE_transmitter_SENDPARITY   4
21 #define STATE_transmitter_INIT      5
22 #define STATE_transmitter_STOPBIT 6
23 #define STATE_transmitter_STARTBIT   7
24
25 class ComponentState_transmitter_idle : public ComponentState {
26 public:
27    ComponentState_transmitter_idle() _CONST_INIT_SECTION:
          ComponentState(STATE_transmitter_IDLE,TIME_INFINITE) {};
28 };
29
30 class ComponentState_transmitter_readdata : public ComponentState {
31 public:
32    ComponentState_transmitter_readdata() _CONST_INIT_SECTION:
          ComponentState(STATE_transmitter_READDATA,0) {};
33 };
34
35 class ComponentState_transmitter_sendbit : public ComponentState {
36 public:
37    ComponentState_transmitter_sendbit() _CONST_INIT_SECTION:
          ComponentState(STATE_transmitter_SENDBIT,0) {};
38 };
39
```

```cpp
40 class ComponentState_transmitter_sendparity : public ComponentState
      {
41 public:
42    ComponentState_transmitter_sendparity() _CONST_INIT_SECTION:
         ComponentState(STATE_transmitter_SENDPARITY,0) {};
43 };
44
45 class ComponentState_transmitter_init : public ComponentState {
46 public:
47    ComponentState_transmitter_init() _CONST_INIT_SECTION:
         ComponentState(STATE_transmitter_INIT,0) {};
48 };
49
50 class ComponentState_transmitter_stopbit : public ComponentState {
51 public:
52    ComponentState_transmitter_stopbit() _CONST_INIT_SECTION:
         ComponentState(STATE_transmitter_STOPBIT,0) {};
53 };
54
55 class ComponentState_transmitter_startbit : public ComponentState {
56 public:
57    ComponentState_transmitter_startbit() _CONST_INIT_SECTION:
         ComponentState(STATE_transmitter_STARTBIT,0) {};
58 };
59
60 class Atomic_Component_transmitter : public Atomic_Component {
61 public:
62    Atomic_Component_transmitter() _CONST_INIT_SECTION :
63       Atomic_Component(&registerFile.currentState_transmitter),
64       variable_send(&registerFile.variable_transmitter_send),
65       variable_parity(&registerFile.variable_transmitter_parity),
66       variable_bits(&registerFile.variable_transmitter_bits),
67       variable_transmit(&registerFile.variable_transmitter_transmit)
68       { };
69    void reset() const; //override
70    void eventRun() const; //override
71    // Output Ports
72    static Port1Bit* const outport_dataack;
73    static Port1Bit* const outport_tx;
74    // Input Ports
75    static PortU8Bit* const inport_data;
76    // Variables
77    int32_t* const variable_send;
78    int32_t* const variable_parity;
79    int32_t* const variable_bits;
80    int32_t* const variable_transmit;
81 private:
82    // States
83    ComponentState_transmitter_idle const state_idle;
```

```
84   ComponentState_transmitter_readdata const state_readdata;
85   ComponentState_transmitter_sendbit const state_sendbit;
86   ComponentState_transmitter_sendparity const state_sendparity;
87   ComponentState_transmitter_init const state_init;
88   ComponentState_transmitter_stopbit const state_stopbit;
89   ComponentState_transmitter_startbit const state_startbit;
90 };
91
92 #endif /* ATOMIC_COMPONENT_TRANSMITTER_H_ */
```

Listing A.8 Atomic_Component_transmitter class definition C++ source code
for an UART transceiver

```
1 #include "Atomic_Component_transmitter.h"
2
3 void Atomic_Component_transmitter :: reset () const {
4    // Outport init
5    this->outport_dataack->data=0;
6    this->outport_dataack->isActive=false;
7    this->outport_tx->data=0;
8    this->outport_tx->isActive=false;
9    // Variable initialization
10   *variable_send = 0;
11   *variable_parity = 0;
12   *variable_bits = 0;
13   *variable_transmit = 0;
14   // Set Initial State
15   startNewState ((ComponentState * const) &state_init);
16 }
17
18 void Atomic_Component_transmitter :: eventRun () const {
19   this->outport_dataack->isActive = false;
20   this->outport_tx->isActive = false;
21
22   switch (this->current_state->current_state_id) {
23   case STATE_transmitter_IDLE:{ //=state_idle
24     if ( this->inport_data->isActive) {
25       register int tempVariable_send = (this->inport_data->data);
26       register int tempVariable_parity = 0;
27       register int tempVariable_bits = 0;
28       register int tempVariable_transmit = 0;
29       *variable_send = tempVariable_send;
30       *variable_parity = tempVariable_parity;
31       *variable_bits = tempVariable_bits;
32       *variable_transmit = tempVariable_transmit;
33       startNewState ((ComponentState * const) &state_readdata);
34     }
35     break;
```

```cpp
36    }
37
38    case STATE_transmitter_READDATA:{   //=state_readdata
39      if (this->current_state->current_time == 0) {
40        this->outport_dataack->data = 1;
41        this->outport_dataack->isActive = true;
42        this->outport_tx->data = (*variable_transmit);
43        this->outport_tx->isActive = true;
44        register int tempVariable_send = (0<<7 | (*variable_send>>1 &
              127));
45        register int tempVariable_parity = (*variable_send>>0 & 1);
46        register int tempVariable_transmit = (*variable_send>>0 & 1);
47        *variable_send = tempVariable_send;
48        *variable_parity = tempVariable_parity;
49        *variable_transmit = tempVariable_transmit;
50        startNewState((ComponentState * const) &state_startbit);
51      }
52      break;
53    }
54
55    case STATE_transmitter_SENDBIT:{   //=state_sendbit
56      if (this->current_state->current_time == 0 && !this->inport_data
              ->isActive && ( !(((*variable_bits)==8)) )) {
57        this->outport_tx->data = (*variable_transmit);
58        this->outport_tx->isActive = true;
59        register int tempVariable_send = (0<<7 | (*variable_send>>1 &
              127));
60        register int tempVariable_parity = (*variable_parity) ^ (*
              variable_send>>0 & 1);
61        register int tempVariable_bits = ((*variable_bits) + 1);
62        register int tempVariable_transmit = (*variable_send>>0 & 1);
63        *variable_send = tempVariable_send;
64        *variable_parity = tempVariable_parity;
65        *variable_bits = tempVariable_bits;
66        *variable_transmit = tempVariable_transmit;
67        startNewState((ComponentState * const) &state_sendbit);
68      } else
69      if (this->current_state->current_time == 0 && !this->inport_data
              ->isActive && ( (*variable_bits)==8 )) {
70        this->outport_tx->data = (*variable_parity);
71        this->outport_tx->isActive = true;
72        *variable_transmit = 1;
73        startNewState((ComponentState * const) &state_sendparity);
74      } else
75      if (this->current_state->current_time == 0 && !(((*variable_send
              )==8))) {
76        this->outport_tx->data = (*variable_transmit);
77        this->outport_tx->isActive = true;
78        register int tempVariable_send = (0<<7 | (*variable_send>>1 &
```

```
               127));
79        register int tempVariable_parity = (*variable_parity) ^ (*
               variable_send>>0 & 1);
80        register int tempVariable_bits = ((*variable_bits) + 1);
81        register int tempVariable_transmit = (*variable_send>>0 & 1);
82        *variable_send = tempVariable_send;
83        *variable_parity = tempVariable_parity;
84        *variable_bits = tempVariable_bits;
85        *variable_transmit = tempVariable_transmit;
86        startNewState((ComponentState * const) &state_sendbit);
87      } else
88      if (this->current_state->current_time == 0 && (*variable_bits)
               ==8) {
89        this->outport_tx->data = (*variable_parity);
90        this->outport_tx->isActive = true;
91        *variable_transmit = 1;
92        startNewState((ComponentState * const) &state_sendparity);
93      }
94      break;
95    }
96
97    case STATE_transmitter_SENDPARITY:{ //=state_sendparity
98      if (this->current_state->current_time == 0) {
99        this->outport_tx->data = (*variable_transmit);
100       this->outport_tx->isActive = true;
101       startNewState((ComponentState * const) &state_stopbit);
102     }
103     break;
104   }
105
106   case STATE_transmitter_INIT:{ //=state_init
107     if (this->current_state->current_time == 0) {
108       this->outport_tx->data = 1;
109       this->outport_tx->isActive = true;
110       startNewState((ComponentState * const) &state_idle);
111     }
112     break;
113   }
114
115   case STATE_transmitter_STOPBIT:{ //=state_stopbit
116     if (this->current_state->current_time == 0) {
117       startNewState((ComponentState * const) &state_idle);
118     }
119     break;
120   }
121
122   case STATE_transmitter_STARTBIT:{ //=state_startbit
123     if (this->current_state->current_time == 0) {
124       this->outport_tx->data = (*variable_transmit);
```

```cpp
125        this->outport_tx->isActive = true;
126        register int tempVariable_send = (0<<7 | (*variable_send>>1 &
               127));
127        register int tempVariable_parity = (*variable_parity) ^ (*
               variable_send>>0 & 1);
128        register int tempVariable_bits = ((*variable_bits) + 1);
129        register int tempVariable_transmit = (*variable_send>>0 & 1);
130        *variable_send = tempVariable_send;
131        *variable_parity = tempVariable_parity;
132        *variable_bits = tempVariable_bits;
133        *variable_transmit = tempVariable_transmit;
134        startNewState((ComponentState * const) &state_sendbit);
135      }
136      break;
137    }
138  }
139 #ifdef DEBUG
140    xil_printf("transmitter:_STATE=%d,%d\r\n", (int) this->
             current_state->current_state_id, (int) this->current_state->
             current_time);
141    if (this->inport_data->isActive)
142      xil_printf("In-Event_'data'=0x%X\r\n", (int) this->inport_data->
               data);
143    if (this->outport_dataack->isActive)
144      xil_printf("Out-Event_'dataack'=0x%X\r\n", (int) this->
               outport_dataack->data);
145    if (this->outport_tx->isActive)
146      xil_printf("Out-Event_'tx'=0x%X\r\n", (int) this->outport_tx->
               data);
147 #endif /* DEBUG */
148 }
```

APPENDIX B

List of Publications

1. Ralf Laue, **H. Gregor Molter**, Felix Rieder, Kartik Saxena, and Sorin A. Huss. A Novel Multiple Core Co-Processor Architecture for Efficient Server-based Public Key Cryptographic Applications. In *IEEE Computer Society Annual Symposium on VLSI*, Montpellier, France, April 2008.

2. **H. Gregor Molter**. *Kryptographischer Coprozessor für Server: Effiziente und flexible Multi-Core-Architektur für Server als System-on-a-Chip*. VDM Verlag Dr. Müller, August 2008.

3. Falko Strenzke, Erik Tews, **H. Gregor Molter**, Raphael Overbeck, and Abdulhadi Shoufan. Side Channels in the McEliece PKC. In *Int. Workshop on Post-Quantum Cryptography (PQCrypto 2008)*, number 5299/2008 in Lecture Notes in Computer Science, pages 216–229, October 2008.

4. **H. Gregor Molter**, Hui Shao, Henning Sudbrock, Sorin A. Huss, and Heiko Mantel. Designing a Coprocessor for Interrupt Handling on an FPGA. Technical Report TUD-CS-2008103, Modellierung und Analyse von Informationssystemen & Integrierte Schaltungen und Systeme, December 2008.

5. Felix Madlener, **H. Gregor Molter**, and Sorin A. Huss. SC-DEVS: An efficient SystemC Extension for the DEVS Model of Computation. In *ACM/IEEE Design Automation and Test in Europe (DATE'09)*, April 2009.

6. Abdulhadi Shoufan, Thorsten Wink, **H. Gregor Molter**, Sorin A. Huss, and Falko Strenzke. A Novel Processor Architecture for McEliece Cryptosystem and FPGA Platforms. In *20th IEEE International Conference on Application-specific Systems, Architectures and Processors*, July 2009.

7. **H. Gregor Molter**, Kei Ogata, Erik Tews, and Ralf-Philipp Weinmann. An Efficient FPGA Implementation for an DECT Brute-Force Attacking Scenario. In *5th IEEE International Conference on Wireless and Mobile Communications (ICWMC 2009)*, pages 82–86, Los Alamitos, CA, USA, August 2009. IEEE Computer Society.

8. **H. Gregor Molter**, André Seffrin, and Sorin A. Huss. DEVS2VHDL: Automatic Transformation of XML-specified DEVS Model of Computation into Synthesiz-

able VHDL Code. In *12th IEEE Forum on Specification and Design Languages (FDL 2009), Sophia Antipolis, France*, September 2009.

9. **H. Gregor Molter**, Felix Madlener, and Sorin A. Huss. A System Level Design Flow for Embedded Systems based on Model of Computation Mappings. In *4th IFAC Workshop on Discrete-Event System Design (DESDes'09)*, October 2009.

10. Abdulhadi Shoufan, Falko Strenzke, **H. Gregor Molter**, and Marc Stöttinger. A Timing Attack Against Patterson Algorithm in the McEliece PKC. In *12th International Conference on Information Security and Cryptology (ICISC'09)*, Lecture Notes in Computer Science, December 2009.

11. Abdulhadi Shoufan, Thorsten Wink, **H. Gregor Molter**, Sorin A. Huss, and Eike Kohnert. A Novel Cryptoprocessor Architecture for the McEliece Public-Key Cryptosystem. *IEEE Transactions on Computers*, 59.:1133–1546, May 2010. Featured as spotlight paper on the IEEE Transactions on Computers website in November 2010.

12. Alexander Biedermann and **H. Gregor Molter**, editors. *Design Methodologies for Secure Embedded Systems*, volume 78. of *Lecture Notes in Electrical Engineering*. Springer, Berlin, Germany, November 2010.

13. **H. Gregor Molter**, Marc Stöttinger, Abdulhadi Shoufan, and Falko Strenzke. A Simple Power Analysis Attack on a McEliece Cryptoprocessor. *Journal of Cryptographic Engineering*, 1.:29–36, January 2011.

14. Abdulhadi Shoufan, Nico Huber, and **H. Gregor Molter**. A Novel Cryptoprocessor Architecture for Chained Merkle Signature Scheme. *Microprocessors and Microsystems, Embedded Hardware Design, Elsevier*, 35.:34–47, February 2011.

15. **H. Gregor Molter**, André Seffrin, and Sorin A. Huss. State Space Optimization within the DEVS Model of Computation for Timing Efficiency. In *19th IEEE/IFIP International Conference on VLSI and System-on-Chip (VLSI-SoC'11), Hong Kong, China*, pages 422–427, Hong Kong, China, October 2011.

16. **H. Gregor Molter** and Sorin A. Huss. The DEVS Model of Computation - A Foundation for a Novel Embedded Systems Design Methodology. In *7th IEEE International Conference on Computer Engineering and Systems (ICCES'11)*, pages xxi–xxvi, Cairo, Egypt, November 2011.

17. Marc Stöttinger, **H. Gregor Molter**, and Sorin A. Huss. Acceleration of Hypotheses Matrix Generation for DPA Attacks. In *IEEE/ACM Design, Automation and Test in Europe, DATE'12, University Booth, Dresden Germany*, March 2012.

18. **H. Gregor Molter**, Johannes Kohlmann, and Sorin A. Huss. Automated Generation of Embedded Systems Software from timed DEVS MoC Specifications. To appear in *15th Euromicro Conference on Digital System Design (DSD'12)*, September 2012.

APPENDIX C

List of Supervised Theses

1. Nico Huber. Quantenresistente Kryptograhieverfahren: Entwurf und Implementierung einer Hardware-Architektur des Merkle-Signaturverfahrens, February 2009. Bachelor Thesis.

2. Kei Ogata. Implementierung eines Brute-Force-Kodebrechers, January 2009. Diploma Thesis.

3. Andre Seffrin. VHDL Generator für DEVS Modelle, May 2009. Diploma Thesis.

4. Thorsten Wink. Quantenresistente Kryptograhieverfahren, January 2009. Bachelor Thesis.

5. Martin Feldmann. Kryptographischer Coprozessor für Serversysteme: Effiziente und flexible Multi-Core-Architektur als System-on-a-Chip inklusive OpenSSL Integration, February 2010. Master Thesis.

6. Yanmin Guo. DEVS Modell Editor für SystemC Simulation, January 2010. Diploma Thesis.

7. Nabil Sayegh. Sichere Kommunikation in eingebetteten Systemen am Beispiel eines Quadrokopters, June 2010. Diploma Thesis.

8. Johannes Kohlmann. Generierung eingebetteter Systeme aus DEVS-Modellen, April 2011. Master Thesis.

9. Kiril Nastev. Development of a Compiler for the DEVS Processor Platform, January 2012. Bachelor Thesis.

References

[ABZ92]   A.L. Ambler, M.M. Burnett, and B.A. Zimmerman. Operational versus Definitional: A Perspective on Programming Paradigms. *Computer*, 25(9):28–43, 1992.

[AJ74]   A.V. Aho and S.C. Johnson. LR parsing. *ACM Computing Surveys (CSUR)*, 6(2):99–124, 1974.

[Alp10]   Alpha Data. *ADM-XRC-6T1*, February 2010. Available from: http://www.alpha-data.com/pdfs/adm-xrc-6t1.pdf, Last checked: Feb. 29, 2012.

[BDB⁺10] David C. Black, Jack Donovan, Bill Bunton, and Anna Keist. *SystemC: From the Ground Up, Second Edition*. Springer, 2010.

[BKV04]   C.V. Bobeanu, E.J.H. Kerckhoffs, and H. Van Landeghem. Modeling of discrete event systems: A holistic and incremental approach using Petri nets. *ACM Transactions on Modeling and Computer Simulation (TOMACS)*, 14(4):389–423, 2004.

[BLL⁺05] C. Brooks, E.A. Lee, X. Liu, S. Neuendorffer, and Y. Zhao. Heterogeneous Concurrent Modeling and Design in Java. *Memorandum UCB/ERL M05/21*, July 2005.

[BV01]   J.S. Bolduc and H. Vangheluwe. The Modelling and Simulation Package PythonDEVS for Classical Hierarchical DEVS. Technical report, MSDL technical report MSDL-TR-2001-01, McGill University, 2001.

[Chr10]   Chrontel. *CH7301C DVI Transmitter Device (Rev. 1.5)*, March 2010. Available from: http://www.chrontel.com/pdf/7301ds.pdf, Last checked: Feb. 21, 2012.

[CN01]   Bruce Childers and Tarun Nakra. Reordering Memory Bus Transactions for Reduced Power Consumption. In Jack Davidson and Sang Min, editors, *Languages, Compilers, and Tools for Embedded Systems*, volume 1985 of *Lecture Notes in Computer Science*, pages 146–161. Springer Berlin / Heidelberg, 2001.

[CSH07]   Christopher Claus, Walter Stechele, and Andreas Herkersdorf. Autovision - A Run-time Reconfigurable MPSoC Architecture for Future Driver Assistance Systems. *it - Information Technology*, 49(3):181–186, 2007.

[DEV11]   DEVS Standardization Group. DEVS tools, September 2011. Available from: http://cell-devs.sce.carleton.ca/devsgroup/?q=node/8, Last checked: Sep. 01, 2011.

[DFL74]   J. Dennis, J. Fosseen, and J. Linderman. Data Flow Schemas. In Andrei Ershov and Valery A. Nepomniaschy, editors, *International Symposium on Theoretical Programming*, volume 5 of *Lecture Notes in Computer Science*, pages 187–216. Springer Berlin / Heidelberg, 1974. DOI: 10.1007/3-540-06720-5_15.

[Dig99]   Digital Display Working Group. *Digital Visual Interface Revision 1.0*, April 1999. Available from: http://www.ddwg.org/lib/dvi_10.pdf, Last checked: Feb. 21, 2012.

[Dij76]   E.W. Dijkstra. *A Discipline of Programming*. Prentice-Hall Series in Automatic Computation. Prentice-Hall, 1976.

[DP06]   D. Densmore and R. Passerone. A platform-based taxonomy for ESL design. *Design & Test of Computers, IEEE*, 23(5):359–374, 2006.

[DV02]   J. De Lara and H. Vangheluwe. Using AToM^3 as a Meta-CASE Tool. In *Proceedings of the 4th International Conference on Enterprise Information Systems (ICEIS)*, pages 642–649, 2002.

[EMD09]   Wolfgang Ecker, Wolfgang Müller, and Rainer Dömer, editors. *Hardware-dependent Software: Principles and Practice*. Springer, 2009.

[FLN06]   T. Filiba, M.K. Leung, and V. Nagpal. VHDL Code Generation in the Ptolemy II Environment. Technical report, Electrical Engineering and Computer Sciences, UC Berkeley, 2006.

[Fre11]   Free Software Foundation, Inc. *Bison 2.5*, May 2011. Available from: http://www.gnu.org/software/bison/manual/html_node/index.html, Last checked: Feb. 14, 2012.

[GHP+09] A. Gerstlauer, C. Haubelt, A.D. Pimentel, T.P. Stefanov, D.D. Gajski, and J. Teich. Electronic System-Level Synthesis Methodologies. *Computer-Aided Design of Integrated Circuits and Systems, IEEE Transactions on*, 28(10):1517–1530, 2009.

[GS93]   David Gries and Fred B. Schneider. *A Logical Approach to Discrete Math.* Springer, 1993.

[Har87]   David Harel. StateCharts: A Visual Formalism for Complex Systems. *Science of Computer Programming*, 8(3):231 – 274, 1987.

[HMV04]   Darrel Hankerson, Alfred J. Menezes, and Scott Vanstone. *Guide to Elliptic Curve Cryptography*. Springer, 2004.

[HOS+07] Andreas Herrholz, Frank Oppenheimer, Andreas Schallenberg, Wolfgang Nebel, Christoph Grimm, Markus Damm, Fernando Herrera,

Eugenio Villar, Ingo Sander, Axel Jantsch, and Anne-Marie Fouilliart. ANDRES - ANalysis and Design of run-time REconfigurable, heterogeneous Systems . In *Design, Automation and Test in Europe (DATE'07)*, April 2007.

[HV07]   Fernando Herrera and Eugenio Villar. A Framework for Heterogeneous Specification and Design of Electronic Embedded Systems in SystemC. *ACM Trans. Des. Autom. Electron. Syst.*, 12(3):1–31, 2007.

[HZ09]   M.H. Hwang and B.P. Zeigler. Reachability Graph of Finite and Deterministic DEVS Networks. *Automation Science and Engineering, IEEE Transactions on*, 6(3):468–478, June 2009.

[IEE08]   IEEE and Open Group. The Open Group Base Specifications Issue 7. *IEEE Std. 1003.1-2008*, 2008. Available from: http://pubs.opengroup. org/onlinepubs/9699919799/, Last checked: Oct. 19, 2011.

[Jan04]   Axel Jantsch. *Modeling Embedded Systems and SoC's*. Morgan Kaufmann, San Diego, 2004.

[JK06]   V. Janoušek and E. Kironskỳ. Exploratory Modeling with SmallDEVS. In *Proceedings of the 20th annual European Simulation and Modelling Conference*, pages 122–126, 2006.

[Knu64]   Donald E. Knuth. Backus Normal Form vs. Backus Naur Form. *Commun. ACM*, 7:735–736, December 1964.

[Knu98]   Donald E. Knuth. *The Art of Computer Programming, Volume 2 (3rd Edition): Seminumerical Algorithms*. Addison-Wesley Longman Publishing Co., Inc., Boston, MA, USA, 1998.

[Kob87]   N. Koblitz. Elliptic curve cryptosystems. *Mathematics of Computation*, 48:203–209, 1987.

[Lau09]   Ralf Laue. *Efficient and Flexible Cryptographic Co-Processor Architecture for Server Application*. PhD thesis, Technische Universität Darmstadt, February 2009. Available from: http://tuprints.ulb.tu-darmstadt.de/ 1327/, Last checked: Feb. 27, 2012.

[Lee08]   Edward A. Lee. Cyber physical systems: Design challenges. *Object-Oriented Real-Time Distributed Computing, IEEE International Symposium on*, 0:363–369, 2008.

[Lee09]   Edward A. Lee. Finite State Machines and Modal Models in Ptolemy II. Technical Report UCB/EECS-2009-151, EECS Department, University of California, Berkeley, Nov 2009.

[LEH+08]   T. Lager, I. Expert, M. Helbing, R. Hosn, TV Raman, and K. Reifenrath. State Chart XML (SCXML): State Machine Notation for Control Abstraction. 2008. Available from: http://stu.w3.org/TR/2008/ WD-scxml-20080516/, Last checked: Mar. 19, 2009.

[Lev09]   John Levine. *Flex & Bison: Text Processing Tools*. O'Reilly Media, 2009.

[LKH⁺96]   Y.M. Lee, H.B. Kim, J.S. Hong, and K.H. Park. Translation from DEVS Models to Synthesizable VHDL Programs. In *IEEE TENCON. Digital Signal Processing Applications (TENCON'96)*, volume 1, 1996.

[LMR⁺08]   Ralf Laue, H. Gregor Molter, Felix Rieder, Kartik Saxena, and Sorin A. Huss. A Novel Multiple Core Co-Processor Architecture for Efficient Server-based Public Key Cryptographic Applications. In *IEEE Computer Society Annual Symposium on VLSI*, Montpellier, France, April 2008.

[LS10]   C.E. LaForest and J.G. Steffan. Efficient Multi-Ported Memories for FPGAs. In *Proceedings of the 18th annual ACM/SIGDA International Symposium on Field Programmable Gate Arrays*, pages 41–50. ACM, 2010.

[LSV98]   E.A. Lee and A. Sangiovanni-Vincentelli. A Framework for Comparing Models of Computation. *Computer-Aided Design of Integrated Circuits and Systems, IEEE Transactions on*, 17(12):1217–1229, 1998.

[Mar07]   Marschner, Alex. *FSL 2 Serial Peripheral*, 2007. Available from: http://opencores.org/project,fsl2serial, Last checked: Dec. 29, 2011.

[MC07]   K.L.P. Mishra and N. Chandrasekaran. *Theory of Computer Science: Automata, Languages and Computation*. Prentice-Hall of India Pvt. Ltd., 2007. 3rd Revision.

[MH11]   H. Gregor Molter and Sorin A. Huss. The DEVS Model of Computation - A Foundation for a Novel Embedded Systems Design Methodology. In *7th IEEE International Conference on Computer Engineering and Systems (ICCES'11)*, Cairo, Egypt, November 2011.

[MHB09]   Felix Madlener, Sorin A. Huss, and Alexander Biedermann. RecDEVS: A Comprehensive Model of Computation for Dynamically Reconfigurable Hardware Systems. In *4th IFAC Workshop on Discrete-Event System Design (DESDes'09)*, October 2009.

[Mil86]   V. Miller. Use of elliptic curves in cryptography. *Lecture Notes in Computer Science*, 218:417–426, 1986.

[MKH12]   H. Gregor Molter, Johannes Kohlmann, and Sorin A. Huss. Automated Generation of Embedded Systems Software from timed DEVS MoC Specifications. To appear in *15th Euromicro Conference on Digital System Design (DSD'12)*, September 2012.

[MMH09a]   Felix Madlener, H. Gregor Molter, and Sorin A. Huss. SC-DEVS: An efficient SystemC Extension for the DEVS Model of Computation. In *ACM/IEEE Design Automation and Test in Europe (DATE'09)*, April 2009.

[MMH09b]   H. Gregor Molter, Felix Madlener, and Sorin A. Huss. A System Level Design Flow for Embedded Systems based on Model of Computation

Mappings. In *4th IFAC Workshop on Discrete-Event System Design (DES-Des'09)*, October 2009.

[MMP10]   L.G. Murillo, M. Mura, and M. Prevostini. MDE Support for HW/SW Codesign: A UML-based Design Flow. *Advances in Design Methods from Modeling Languages for Embedded Systems and SoC's*, pages 19–37, 2010.

[Mol08]   H. Gregor Molter. *Kryptographischer Coprozessor für Server: Effiziente und flexible Multi-Core-Architektur für Server als System-on-a-Chip*. VDM Verlag Dr. Müller, August 2008.

[MSH09]   H. Gregor Molter, André Seffrin, and Sorin A. Huss. DEVS2VHDL: Automatic Transformation of XML-specified DEVS Model of Computation into Synthesizable VHDL Code. In *12th IEEE Forum on Specification and Design Languages (FDL 2009)*, September 2009.

[MSH11]   H. Gregor Molter, André Seffrin, and Sorin A. Huss. State Space Optimization within the DEVS Model of Computation for Timing Efficiency. In *19th IFIP/IEEE International Conference on Very Large Scale Integration (VLSI-SoC'11)*, Hong Kong, China, October 2011.

[MvOV96] A. Menezes, P. van Oorschot, and S. Vanstone. *Handbook of Applied Cryptography*. CRC Press, 1996. Available from: http://www.cacr.math.uwaterloo.ca/hac/, Last checked: Mar. 3rd, 2012.

[MWH10]   Felix Madlener, Julia Weingart, and Sorin A. Huss. Verification of Dynamically Reconfigurable Embedded Systems by Model Transformation Rules. In *4th IEEE/ACM International Conference on Hardware-Software Codesign and System Synthesis (CODES+ISSS 2010)*, October 2010.

[Nat99]   National Institute of Standards and Technology. *Recommended Elliptic Curves for Federal Government use*, July 1999. Available from: http://csrc.nist.gov/groups/ST/toolkit/documents/dss/NISTReCur.pdf, Last checked: Mar. 11th, 2012.

[Nat09]   National Institute of Standards and Technology. *Digital Signature Standard (FIPS PUB 186-3)*, July 2009. Available from: http://csrc.nist.gov/publications/fips/fips186-3/fips_186-3.pdf, Last checked: Mar. 11th, 2012.

[NDA10]   Mara Nikolaidou, Vassilis Dalakas, and Dimosthenis Anagnostopoulos. Integrating Simulation Capabilities in SysML using DEVS. In *Proceedings of IEEE Systems Conference 2010*, 2010.

[Nok11]   Nokia Corporation. *Qt – Online Reference Documentation*, 2011. Available from: http://doc.qt.nokia.com/, Last checked: Feb. 16, 2012.

[Nut99]   J. Nutaro. ADEVS (A Discrete EVent System simulator) C++ library, 1999. Available from: http://www.ornl.gov/~1qn/adevs/, Last checked: Sep. 01, 2011.

[NXP12]   NXP Semiconductors. *UM10204 – I²C-Bus Specification and User Manual*, February 2012. Available from: http://www.nxp.com/acrobat_download/usermanuals/UM10204_3.pdf, Last checked: Feb. 21, 2012.

[PD84]   Thomas Porter and Tom Duff. Compositing Digital Images. In *Proceedings of the 11th annual Conference on Computer Graphics and Interactive Techniques*, SIGGRAPH '84, pages 253–259, New York, NY, USA, 1984. ACM.

[PNA⁺11]   Sumet Prabhavat, Hiroki Nishiyama, Nirwan Ansari, and Nei Kato. Effective Delay-Controlled Load Distribution over Multipath Networks. *IEEE Transation on Parallel and Distributed Systems*, 22(10):1730–1741, 2011.

[PUS11]   M. Petzold, O. Ullrich, and E. Speckenmeyer. Dynamic Distributed Simulation of DEVS Models on the OSGi Service Platform. *Proceedings of ASIM 2011*, 2011.

[RDM⁺09]   J.L. Risco-Martín, J.M. De La Cruz, S. Mittal, and B.P. Zeigler. eUDEVS: Executable UML with DEVS theory of modeling and simulation. *Simulation*, 85(11-12):750, 2009.

[RMZ⁺07]   J.L. Risco-Martín, S. Mittal, B.P. Zeigler, and M. Jesús. From UML Statecharts to DEVS State Machines using XML. In *IEEE/ACM conference on Multi-paradigm Modeling and Simulation, Nashville, September*, 2007.

[RSA02]   RSA Laboratories. PKCS #1 v2.1: RSA Cryptography Standard. Technical report, June 2002. Available from: ftp://ftp.rsasecurity.com/pub/pkcs/pkcs-1/pkcs-1v2-1.pdf, Last checked: Feb. 29, 2012.

[Rus11]   A. Rushton. *VHDL for Logic Synthesis*. John Wiley & Sons, 2011.

[Sim00]   Simulation Interoperability Standards Committee (SISC). IEEE Standard for Modeling and Simulation (M&S) High Level Architecture (HLA) - Framework and Rules. *IEEE Std. 1516-2000*, 2000.

[SJ04]   I. Sander and A. Jantsch. System Modeling and Transformational Design Refinement in ForSyDe. *IEEE Transactions on Computer-Aided Design of Integrated Circuits and Systems*, 23(1):17–32, 2004.

[SS04]   H.S. Sarjoughian and R. Singh. Building Simulation Modeling Environments using Systems Theory and Software Architecture Principles. In *Proceedings of the Advanced Simulation Technology Conference (ASTC'04)*, pages 235–240, April 2004.

[SV11]   Reehan Shaikh and Hans Vangheluwe. Transforming UML2.0 class diagrams and statecharts to atomic DEVS. In *Proceedings of the 2011 Symposium on Theory of Modeling & Simulation: DEVS Integrative M&S Symposium*, TMS-DEVS '11, pages 205–212, San Diego, CA, USA, 2011.

[Sys06]   IEEE Standard System C Language Reference Manual. *IEEE Std 1666-2005*, pages 1–423, 2006.

[Ver96]   IEEE Standard Hardware Description Language Based on Verilog (R) Hardware Description Language. *IEEE Std 1364-1996*, 1996.

[Vhd87]   IEEE Standard VHDL Language Reference Manual. *IEEE Std 1076-1987*, pages 1–218, 1987.

[VM07]   Will Estes Vern Paxson and John Millaway. *Lexical Analysis With Flex*, September 2007. Available from: http://flex.sourceforge.net/manual/, Last checked: Feb. 14, 2012.

[Wai09]   Gabriel A. Wainer. *Discrete-Event Modeling and Simulation: A Practitioner's Approach (Computational Analysis, Synthesis, and Design of Dynamic Systems)*. CRC Press, 2009.

[WRZ+11]   S. Wildermann, F. Reimann, D. Ziener, and J. Teich. Symbolic Design Space Exploration for Multi-Mode Reconfigurable Systems. In *Hardware/Software Codesign and System Synthesis (CODES+ ISSS), 2011 Proceedings of the 9th International Conference on*, pages 129–138, October 2011.

[WWZ+11]   Wenguang Wang, Weiping Wang, Yifan Zhu, and Qun Li. Service-oriented Simulation Framework: An Overview and Unifying Methodology. *SIMULATION*, 87(3):221–252, 2011.

[Xil09a]   Xilinx, Inc. *Xilinx DS100 Virtex-5 Family Overview*, 2009. Available from: http://www.xilinx.com/support/documentation/data_sheets/ds100.pdf, Last checked: Dec. 29, 2011.

[Xil09b]   Xilinx, Inc. *XST User Guide*, 2009. Available from: http://www.xilinx.com/support/documentation/sw_manuals/xilinx11/xst.pdf, Last checked: Jan. 04, 2012.

[Xil10a]   Xilinx, Inc. *Xilinx DS572 LogiCORE IP XPS Interrupt Controller (v2.01a)*, 2010. Available from: http://www.xilinx.com/support/documentation/ip_documentation/xps_intc.pdf, Last checked: Jan. 11, 2012.

[Xil10b]   Xilinx, Inc. *Xilinx DS573 LogiCORE IP XPS Timer/Counter (v1.02a)*, 2010. Available from: http://www.xilinx.com/support/documentation/ip_documentation/xps_timer.pdf, Last checked: Jan. 11, 2012.

[Xil11a]   Xilinx, Inc. *Xilinx DS571 LogiCORE IP XPS UART Lite (v1.02.a)*, 2011. Available from: http://www.xilinx.com/support/documentation/ip_documentation/xps_uartlite/v1_02_a/xps_uartlite.pdf, Last checked: Dec. 29, 2011.

[Xil11b]   Xilinx, Inc. *Xilinx University Program XUPV5-LX110T Development System*, 2011. Available from: http://www.xilinx.com/univ/xupv5-lx110t.htm, Last checked: Dec. 29, 2011.

[Xil12]   Xilinx, Inc. *OS and Libraries Document Collection*, January 2012. Available from: http://www.xilinx.com/support/documentation/sw_manuals/xilinx13_4/oslib_rm.pdf, Last checked: Feb. 27, 2012.

[YHS10]   H. Youness, M. Hassan, and A. Salem. A Design Space Exploration Methodology for Allocating Task Precedence Graphs to Multi-Core System Architectures. In *Microelectronics (ICM), 2010 International Conference on*, pages 260–263, June 2010.

[YWH+10] H. Youness, A.M. Wahdan, M. Hassan, A. Salem, M. Moness, K. Sakanushi, Y. Takeuchi, and M. Imai. Efficient partitioning technique on multiple cores based on optimal scheduling and mapping algorithm. In *Circuits and Systems (ISCAS), Proceedings of 2010 IEEE International Symposium on*, pages 3729–3732, December 2010.

[ZHS99]   B.P. Zeigler, S.B. Hall, and H.S. Sarjoughian. Exploiting HLA and DEVS to Promote Interoperability and Reuse in Lockheed's Corporate Environment. *Simulation*, 73(5):288, 1999.

[ZKP00]   Bernard P. Zeigler, Tag Gon Kim, and Herbert Praehofer. *Theory of Modeling and Simulation*. Academic Press, Inc., 2000.

Printed by Publishers' Graphics LLC
MO20130206.19.28.245